GENERAL
BUSINESS

비즈니스 일상 영어

Giovanna Kim

- 영국 Sheffield-Hallam University 경영학, 회계학 학사
- 영국 University of London에서 영문학 학사
- 영국 Cambridge University ESOL Certificate 취득
- Sangwoo Co.에서 협상가 및 번역가로 활동
- SK증권, 샘스(SAMS), 아산 병원에서 사내 영어 교육 담당
- Brown Education, English Vine Education R&D 팀장
- YBM ELS 학원 회화 및 비즈니스 전문 강사
- 현재 MI International Trading Co. 운영
- 저서 및 감수서 : Oxford University Press, 능률교육, YBM Premier Series, YBM Test, YBM Test Prep, YBM Tourism, YBM Accounting, English Vine Series, Junior Brown Series 등

English for Business Communication

General Business 비즈니스 일상 영어

지은이 Giovanna Kim
펴낸이 정규도
펴낸곳 (주)다락원

초판 1쇄 발행 2008년 7월 18일
2판 1쇄 발행 2019년 11월 29일
2판 5쇄 발행 2023년 9월 1일

편집총괄 장의연
책임편집 권경현
표지 디자인 하태호
본문 디자인 HADA 장선숙
전산 편집 HADA 장선숙
삽화 김인화
사진 shutterstock

다락원 경기도 파주시 문발로 211
내용문의: (02)736-2031 내선 523
구입문의: (02)736-2031 내선 250~252
Fax: (02)732-2037
출판등록 1977년 9월 16일 제406-2008-000007호

ISBN 978-89-277-0117-0 13740

http://www.darakwon.co.kr

• 다락원 홈페이지를 방문하시면 상세한 출판정보와 함께 여러 도서의 동영상강좌, MP3자료 등 다양한 어학 정보를 얻으실 수 있습니다.

GENERAL BUSINESS
비즈니스 일상 영어

Giovanna Kim

DARAKWON

Preface

I have been teaching English at the largest language school in Korea for a number of years and in that time I have learned that there are many people out there who wanted to study business English for many different reasons. Unfortunately for them, they have not been able to do so because they did not have the time to study, were not confident enough to join a class, or simply wished to work on their own but could not find the right text for them.

The book is designed for those interested in self-study as well as for students of language classes. Self-study students will find that the lesson layout is set out to maximize the efficiency and convenience of those who have a very busy working life but who would still like to study business English. Students in language classrooms and in online programs will find that the opportunities for speaking meet their need for practice in authentic business scenarios.

My only wish now after having finished writing <General Business> is that those people who want to study business English but have not yet found the right book for them, or the time to study, will benefit from this book and talk business fluently with absolute confidence! I owe many deep debts of gratitude to the people who supported me through the process of writing this book. First and foremost, I would like to thank my husband and my brothers for the kind and undying support during those times when I doubted both my ability, and capacity, to carry out such a task. I would also like to thank Darakwon for giving me the opportunity and the editors for providing me with the help necessary to completing this book. Finally, I would like to dedicate this book to my parents whose loving spirit pervades this work from beginning to end.

Giovanna Kim

한국의 규모 있는 어학원에서 여러 해 영어를 가르쳐오면서, 많은 직장인이 여러 가지 이유로 비즈니스 영어를 공부하고자 한다는 걸 알게 됐습니다. 하지만 안타깝게도 시간이 없어서, 수업에 참여할 용기가 없어서, 혹은 혼자서 공부해 보고자 했지만 적절한 교재를 찾지 못해서 큰 진전을 보지 못하는 경우를 많이 봅니다.

그래서 이 책은 비즈니스 어학 강좌용 교재로 뿐만 아니라, 독학하고자 하는 이들에게도 적합하도록 구현되었습니다. 바쁜 일상을 지내는 이들도 비즈니스 영어를 공부하고자 한다면 누구나 효율성을 극대화하여 편리하게 학습할 수 있도록 구성하였고, 학원이나 온라인을 통해 비즈니스 강좌를 듣는 분들에게는 실제적인 비즈니스 시나리오를 통해 스피킹 연습을 할 수 있는 충분한 기회를 제공해 주고 있습니다. 아무쪼록 많은 이들에게 이 책이 유익하게 작용하여 유창한 비즈니스 영어를 구사하는 동시에 자신감 또한 크게 갖길 바랍니다.

이 책을 집필하는 과정 전반에 걸쳐 저를 지지해준 많은 분께 깊은 감사를 표하고 싶습니다. 먼저, 비즈니스 교재를 쓰면서 어려움이 있을 때마다 아낌없는 지원과 도움을 준 남편과 오빠들에게 큰 고마움을 전합니다. 그리고 이 책을 구현하는 데 중요한 여러 도움을 준 편집자분들과 집필 기회를 준 출판사 다락원에도 감사를 전합니다. 끝으로, 작업 내내 저의 정신적 지주가 되어주셨던 제 부모님께 이 책을 바칩니다.

지오바나 김

Contents

PART 4 해외 출장 Business Trip

SPECIAL PART 비즈니스 이메일 Business E-mail

Overview

PART 1 비즈니스 전화 Business Telephoning

Week	Title	Overview
WEEK 01	전화 걸고 받기 Making and Answering a Call	전화 관련 기본 어휘 익히기 to know basic vocabulary for telephone 전화 걸고 받기 to make & answer a call 전화 바꿔주기 to transfer a call
WEEK 02	메시지 남기고 받기 Leaving and Taking Messages	전화를 받을 수 없는 이유 말하기 to say why he or she is not in 언제 통화가 가능한지 묻기 to ask when he or she is available 메시지 남기고 받기 to leave or take a message
WEEK 03	잘못 걸린 전화와 자동응답기 Wrong Calls and Answering Machine	통화를 하려는 사람 찾기 to look for someone 잘못 걸린 전화에 대응하기 to respond to the wrong number 자동응답기에 용건 남기기 to leave a message to the answering machine
PLUS WEEK	통화 중 문제 발생과 국제전화 Problems with the Phone and International Calls	전화기 문제에 대처하기 when having problems with the phone 전화 통화 다음으로 미루기 to get back to someone later 국제전화 걸기 to make international calls

PART 2 사무실에서의 일상 업무 Daily Routines at the Office

Week	Title	Overview
WEEK 04	미팅 약속 정하기 Making an Arrangement for Meeting	약속 정하기 to set up an appointment 약속 변경하기 to reschedule an appointment 약속 취소하기 to cancel an appointment
WEEK 05	출퇴근 인사와 휴가 신청 Greeting at Work and Asking for Leave	아침 출근인사 하기 to greet in the morning when you get to work 조퇴 사유 말하기 to say why you leave work 휴가 신청하기 to asking for a day off
WEEK 06	감사와 격려 표현하기 Expressing Appreciation and Encouragement	감사와 축하 표기 to show appreciation and to congratulate someone 격려하기 to encourage someone 위로하기 to express one's condolences to someone
PLUS WEEK	사무기기 다루기 Dealing with Office Equipment	사무용품 빌리기 to borrow office supplies 컴퓨터 문제 해결하기 to troubleshoot a computer problem 복사기 문제 해결하기 to troubleshoot a photocopier problem

SPECIAL PART 비즈니스 이메일 Business E-mail

Unit	Title	Overview
UNIT 01	첫 비즈니스 이메일 보내기 Sending a Business E-mail for the First Time	이메일의 목적 말하기 to tell the purpose of e-mail 자기 소개하기 to introduce myself 맺음말 알기 to know the concluding remarks
UNIT 02	첨부파일 보내기 Enclosing an Attachment	첨부파일 보내기 to enclose an attachment 파일 여는 방법 알려주기 to tell how to view the file 유의사항 전달하기 to give previous notice

General Business
Business Telephoning

PART 1
비즈니스 전화

전화 걸고 받기

Making and Answering a Call

Vocabulary & Expressions

전화 Telephone

🔊 전화기 명칭

- **cellular phone** 휴대 전화 (= mobile phone)
- **answering machine** 자동 응답기
- **unlisted number** 전화번호부에 없는 번호 (= ex-directory number)
- **directory assistance** 전화번호 안내
- **extension (number)** 내선 (번호)
- **direct line** 직통 번호 (= hotline)
- **local code** 지역 번호 (= area code)
- **national code** 국가 번호 (= country code)
- **local call** 시내 전화
- **long-distance call** 장거리 전화
- **international call** 국제 전화 (= overseas call)
- **collect call** 수신자부담 전화

receiver 수화기
key pad 숫자판
pound key 샵 버튼 (= hash button)
cord 전화선
star key 별표 키

전화 걸고 받기 Making & Answering a Call

- **call someone** ~에게 전화하다 (= make a call to someone)
- **put A through to B** A의 전화를 B에게 연결해 주다
- **receive a call** 전화를 받다
- **pick up the phone** 수화기를 들다
- **put someone on hold** ~을 기다리게 하다
- **speak to[with] someone** ~와 통화하다

- **wait for a dial tone** 통화음이 울리길 기다리다
- **hang up the phone** 전화를 끊다
- **dial** 다이얼을 돌리다, 전화를 걸다
- **redial** 전화를 다시 걸다
- **hold on** (전화를 끊지 않고) 잠시 기다리다

Useful Expressions

This is Michael calling from New York office.

저는 뉴욕 사무소에서 전화 드리는 마이클**이라고 합니다.**

How can I help you?

무엇을 도와 드릴까요?

Who would you like to speak to?

누구를 바꿔 드릴까요?

May I ask who's calling , please?

전화 거시는 분이 **누구신지** 여쭤봐도 될까요?

Could you put me through to Jessica, please?

제시카 씨를 **바꿔 주시겠어요?**

Vocabulary Check-Up

A Match the meanings on the left with the expressions on the right.

1 전화를 끊다 ·   · ⓐ hang up the phone

2 발신음 ·   · ⓑ unlisted number

3 수신자 부담 전화 ·   · ⓒ dial tone

4 전화번호부에 없는 번호 ·   · ⓓ busy signal

5 통화 중 신호음 ·   · ⓔ collect call

B Fill in the blanks with the given words.

1 전화가 울리네요. 전화 받아주세요.
  ▶ The phone has been ringing. You need to _____ _____ the phone.

2 여보세요, 브라운 씨와 통화하고 싶습니다.
  ▶ Hello, I'd like to _____ _____ Mr. Brown.

3 이 스마트폰 어떻게 사용하는지 알려 주시겠어요?
  ▶ Can you tell me how to use this _____?

4 고객서비스팀 담당자와 통화하고 싶습니다.
  ▶ I would like to speak to the person who is _____ _____ _____
    customer service.

> **Words**
> speak to
> pick up
> smartphone
> in charge of

C Refer to the Korean and fill in the blanks.

1 _____ _____ James Roberts. 저는 제임스 로버츠입니다.

2 Could I have _____ 581, please? 내선 581번 부탁드립니다.

3 May I ask who's _____? 전화 거신 분이 누구신지 여쭤봐도 될까요?

4 _____ on, please, Mr. Roberts. 로버츠 씨, 잠깐만 기다려 주세요.

5 I will _____ you _____. 연결해 드리겠습니다.

I'll transfer your call to her.   그분에게 전화를 돌려 드리겠습니다.

This is she.   전데요. (*남자일 때는 she 대신 he를 쓴다.)

I'd like to speak to the person in charge of accounting.   회계 담당하시는 분과 통화하고 싶은데요.

Hold on, please.   끊지 말고 기다려 주세요.

How can I reach Mr. Baker?   베이커 씨와 통화하려면 어떻게 해야 하나요?

01.mp3

A Good morning. DRK, Sarah Taylor speaking.
   How may I help you?

B Yes, good morning, Ms.Taylor. **¹May I speak to** Mr.
   Smith in the Marketing Department, **please**?

A **²May I ask** who's calling, please?

B **³This is** Lee Minsu **from** KTS.

A Certainly. I will transfer your call now. Wait a moment, sir.

B Sure, I will hold. Thank you.

Pattern Training

1 **May I speak to** [ ], **please?** ~와 통화할 수 있나요?

① Ms. Smith in the QCS Department
② the person who is in charge of the Sales Department
③ Mr. Burnside in the PR Department

▶ 품질관리부의 스미스 씨 / 영업부 담당자 / 홍보실의 번사이드 씨

🔊 비슷한 표현(비격식)
Is Jane there?
제인 있어요?

🔊 비슷한 표현(격식)
Can I speak to Jane, please?
I'd like to speak to Jane, please.
제인과 통화하고 싶은데요.

2 **May I ask** [ ]**?** ~을 여쭤봐도 될까요?

① what this is regarding
② what this is about
③ your name

▶ 용건이 무엇인지 / 무슨 일인지 / 성함

3 **This is** [ ] **from** [ ].
저는 …에 근무하는 ~입니다.

① Sarah, Soft Ltd.
② Rebecca, Sangho International Trade
③ Sean, World Tour Co.

▶ 소프트 주식회사에 근무하는 세라 / 상호 국제 무역에 근무하는 레베카 /
월드투어 사에 근무하는 션

🔊 잠시 대기시키는 표현
Wait a moment.
Hold on, please.
One moment, please.
Just a second, please.
잠깐만 기다려 주세요.

02.mp3

A HM Service, Rachel speaking. What can I do for you?

B [1]**I'd like to speak to** Mr. Robert Digger, **please**.

A One moment, sir. I will put you through.

B (a little later) Sir? [2]**I'm afraid he's** just stepped out.

A Hmm… I shall try to call him a little later then.
Could you tell me what his extension is, please?

B Of course, sir. It's 322.

A Thank you.

Pattern Training

1 **I'd like to speak to** [_____], **please.** ~ 씨와 통화하고 싶습니다.

① Ms. Stacy in the PR Department
② Mr. Ronson in the Administration Department
③ Mr. Parkinson in the HR Department
▶ 홍보부의 스테이스 씨 / 관리부의 론슨 씨 / 인사관리부의 파킨슨 씨

2 **I'm afraid he's** [_____]. 그분은 ~인 것 같은데요.

① at lunch now
② not in this afternoon
③ in a meeting right now
▶ 지금 점심식사 중인 / 오늘 오후에 자리에 안 계신 / 지금 회의 중인

A Fill in the blanks with the given words.

extension	may	back	transfer
afraid	on	reach	how

1 A: Good morning. HM Service. _____ can I help you?

B: My name is Park Jungmin. _____ I speak to Mr. Jones?

안녕하세요. HM 서비스입니다. 무엇을 도와 드릴까요? – 저는 박정민이라고 합니다. 존스 씨와 통화할 수 있을까요?

2 A: I'm _____ he's not here right now.

B: I will call _____ another time then.

그분은 지금 자리에 안 계신 것 같은데요. – 그럼, 나중에 다시 전화 드리겠습니다.

3 A: I will _____ your call. Hold _____, please.

B: Okay. Thank you.

전화를 돌려 드리겠습니다. 잠시만 기다려 주세요. – 네. 감사합니다.

4 A: I'm trying to _____ Mr. Smith. What is his _____?

B: His extension is 307. I'll connect you.

스미스 씨와 통화하고 싶은데요. 내선번호가 어떻게 되나요? – 스미스 씨 내선번호는 307입니다. 연결해 드릴게요.

B Complete the short dialogs.

1

A: 전화 거신 분은 누구시죠? (may / call)

B: This is John Smith calling from the ACE Company.

2

A: 지금 연결해 드리겠습니다. (put through) Hold the line, please.

B: Thank you.

3

A: 그분은 지금 회의 중이신 것 같습니다. (I'm afraid …)

B: I shall try to call him a little later then.

4

A: 어느 분과 통화하시려는 건가요? (try / reach)

B: Is Ms. Johns there? My cell phone says I missed her call.

A Listen to the dialog and check true or false.

03.mp3

	True	False
1 Mr. Park works for ABC Associates.		
2 Mr. Park is not able to come to the phone now.		
3 The caller wants to change the scheduled appointment.		

B Listen to the dialog and answer the questions.

04.mp3

1 Who is the caller?

▶

2 Who does the caller want to speak to?

▶

3 Does the caller know the person's extension?

▶

4 Does the caller leave a message with the personal assistant? Why or why not?

▶

C Listen again and complete the blanks.

04.mp3

Helen: ¹_____ _____, Axa Electronics, Helen Watson speaking. How may I help you?

Sungmin: I'd like to speak to Mr. White, please. I ² _____ _____ _____ _____ though.

Helen: May I ³ _____ _____ _____ _____?

Sungmin: Oh, sorry. This is Kim Sungmin from M.I. International.

Helen: Just a moment, please. I ⁴ _____ _____ _____ _____ _____.

Sungmin: Sure. I'll hold.

Helen: I am sorry, Mr. Kim. But he's ⁵ _____ _____ _____ _____ _____.
          Would you like to leave a message?

Sungmin: That's okay. I will ⁶ _____ _____ _____ _____ _____ _____. Thank you.

Helen: Good day, sir.

메시지 남기고 받기

Leaving and Taking Messages

Vocabulary & Expressions

전화를 받을 수 없는 경우 When He or She Is Not in

- **not be in yet** 출근 전이다
- **step out** 나가다, 외출하다
- **be on another line** 통화 중이다
- **be out to lunch** 점심 식사하러 나가다
- **be in a meeting** 회의 중이다
- **have just left** 방금 퇴근하다
- **be off-duty** 쉬는 날이다
- **have[take] a day off** 하루 휴가를 얻다
- **call in sick** 병가를 내다
- **be on vacation** 휴가 중이다
- **be on a business trip** 출장 중이다
- **be transferred to** ~로 전근가다
- **leave a company** 퇴사하다 (= quit one's job)

철자를 불러주는 법

A: Could you spell your name, please?
성함을 불러주시겠어요?

B: It's f as in Freddie, r as in Romeo, e as in Echo, and d as in Delta. That is Fred.
Freddie의 f, Romeo의 r, Echo의 e, Delta의 d, Fred입니다.

메시지 남기고 받기 Leaving or Taking a Message

- **pass the message on to someone** ~에게 메시지를 전달하다
- **leave a message** 메시지를 남기다
- **take a message** 메시지를 받다
- **double-check** 재확인하다
- **come back / return / be back** 돌아오다

- **repeat** 반복하다
- **read back** (확인하기 위해) 읽어보다
- **call back** 나중에 다시 전화하다
- **return a call** 응답 전화를 하다

Useful Expressions

John is not here right now .	존은 지금 자리에 없습니다.
Can I take a message?	메시지를 받아둘까요?
Would you like to leave a message?	메시지를 남기시겠습니까?
Can I have your name and contact number , please?	성함과 연락처를 불러주시겠어요?
Could you pass the message on to him for me?	그에게 메시지를 전해주시겠어요?

A Match the meanings on the left with the expressions on the right.

1 통화 중이다 · · ⓐ return a call

2 회신 전화를 하다 · · ⓑ be on another line

3 회의 중이다 · · ⓒ be out to lunch

4 하루 쉬다 · · ⓓ be in a meeting

5 점심 먹으러 나가다 · · ⓔ have a day off

B Fill in the blanks with the given words.

1 그녀가 시간 날 때 전화 드리라고 할까요?

▶ May I _____ _____ _____ _____ you when she's free?

2 메시지를 남기시겠습니까?

▶ Would you like to _____ _____ _____?

3 그녀에게 가능한 한 빨리 전화해 달라고 전해주시겠어요?

▶ Could you tell her to call me _____ _____ _____ she can?

4 성함과 연락처를 알려 주시겠어요?

▶ Can I _____ your _____ and _____ _____, please?

Words
as soon as
have one's name
contact number
leave a message
ask someone to call

C Refer to the Korean and fill in the blanks.

1 Could you _____ your name, please? 이름의 철자를 불러주시겠어요?

2 He _____ in sick today. 몸이 아파서 오늘 결근하셨습니다.

3 Could you _____ that, please? 다시 한번 말씀해 주시겠습니까?

4 I'm sorry. He's away on a _____ _____ until Friday. 죄송하지만 금요일까지는 출장 때문에 안 계십니다.

5 Will you _____ it _____ to me to make sure you got everything correct?

맞게 쓰셨는지 확인하려는데요, 다시 좀 읽어주시겠어요?

When will he return? 그는 언제 돌아오나요?

He will be back after lunch. 점심식사 **후에** 돌아올 겁니다.

Could you tell him to call me as soon as he can ? 그에게 **가능한 한 빨리** 전화해 달라고 전해주시겠어요?

Let me read that back. **확인차 읽어보겠습니다.**

Let me check if he's available. 그분이 전화 받으실 수 있는지 확인해 보겠습니다.

05.mp3

A Hello, this is Michelle Aston from Dayton Research. May I speak to Terry Black?

B I'm afraid she's away on a business trip.

A **¹Can you tell me when** she is coming back?

B She won't be back until Monday. May I take a message?

A Yes. **²There has been** a change in our schedule.
So could you have her call me ASAP when she gets back?

B Okay. **³I will pass that on to** Ms. Black **when** she returns.

A I appreciate it.

Pattern Training

1 **Can you tell me when** [_____]?
언제 ~하는지 말씀해 주시겠어요?

① she will be available
② he will return
③ he will be free

▶ 그녀가 통화 가능한지 / 그가 돌아오는지 / 그가 시간이 나는지

🔊 전화 줄 것을 요청하는 표현
▸ Could you **have** her **call** me ASAP?
▸ Could you **tell** her **to give** me **a call** ASAP?
▸ Could you **get** her **to phone** me ASAP?
그녀에게 가능한 한 빨리 제게 **연락 달라고** 전해주시겠어요?

2 **There has been** [_____]. ~가 있었어요.

① a situation in the production line
② a complaint from our client
③ a problem with the delivery

▶ 생산라인 상에 사고 / 고객으로부터의 불만 / 배송에 관련된 문제점

3 **I will pass that on to** [_____] **when** [_____].
그것을 …할 때에 ~에게 전달하겠습니다.

① Ms. Brown, she comes back
② the person who's in charge of the Technical Team, I get a hold of him
③ my manager, I can

▶ 브라운 씨가 돌아오면, 그녀에게 / 기술팀 담당자와 연락이 되면, 그에게 / 가능할 때, 저희 관리자에게

06.mp3

A Would you like to leave a message?

B [1]**Could you tell him to** call me as soon as he can?

A Okay. Can I have your name and contact number, please?

B Certainly, it's Nick Anderson, and my contact number is 07890-255-401.

A Could you spell your name, please?

B Sure. It's N-I-C-K and A-N-D-E-R-S-O-N. N as in November, I as in India, C as in Charlie, K as in Korea…

A Let me double-check that. It's N as in November, I as in India, C as in Charlie, K as in Korea…

B That is correct.

Pattern Training

1   **Could you tell him to** [_____]**?** 그분께 ~하라고 말씀해 주시겠습니까?

① drop by my office sometime this week
② call me back
③ send the completed request form

▶ 이번 주중에 제 사무실에 들러 달라고 / 제게 전화해 달라고 / 작성한 신청서를 보내라고

	Telephone Message
메시지를 받을 사람 →	• To: _____
메시지를 남긴 사람 →	• From: _____
전화의 성격 →	• ☐ called ☐ please call back ☐ will be back
메시지를 남긴 사람의 회사명 →	• Company: _____
전달 내용 →	• Message: _____
연락처 →	• Contact number: _____
메시지를 전달한 사람 →	• Message taken by: _____

* 전화 메시지를 전달할 때는 위의 사항을 정확하게 메모해 두자.

A Fill in the blanks with the given words.

get	back	step out	when	try
pass	leave	call	later	

1 Receiver: Would you like to _____ a message?

Caller: Yes, please have Mr. Brown _____ me as soon as he comes back to the office.

메시지를 남기시겠습니까? – 네, 브라운 씨가 사무실에 돌아오는 대로 저에게 전화해 달라고 전해주세요.

2 Receiver: I'm afraid he's just _____ _____.

Caller: I shall _____ to call him a little _____ then.

지금 막 나가신 것 같아요. – 그럼 잠시 뒤에 다시 걸겠습니다.

3 Caller: _____ is she coming back?

Receiver: She will be _____ next Monday.

그분은 언제 돌아오시나요? – 다음 주 월요일에 돌아오십니다.

4 Caller: Could you _____ him to call me as soon as he can?

Receiver: Sure, I will _____ that on to Mr. Roy.

가능한 한 빨리 제게 전화해 달라고 해주시겠습니까? – 네, 로이 씨에게 전하겠습니다.

B Complete the short dialogs.

1

A: 용건을 전달해 드릴까요? (could / take)
B: Sure. 그가 돌아오는 대로 저에게 전화해 달라고 전해주세요. (tell / call / come back)

2

A: 성함과 연락처를 알려 주시겠어요? (have / contact number)
B: My name is Maria Green, and my phone number is 736-2031.

3

A: When is he expected back?
B: 한 시간 후에 돌아오십니다. (be back)

4

A: 그분은 지금 통화 중이십니다. (on line)
B: I will try to call him later then.

A Listen to the dialog and answer the questions.

07.mp3

1 Who is the caller?

▶ _____

2 Why can't the caller contact with the Ms. White?

▶ _____

3 What is the caller's phone number?

▶ _____

B Listen again and complete the blanks.

07.mp3

Receiver: Good morning. National Trading Company.

Caller: Hello. __1__ _____ ____ _____ to Barbara White.

Receiver: I'm sorry she's in a meeting right now. Would you like __2__ _____ ____ _____?

Caller: Yes. My name is Emma Elite. Please ask Ms. White to __3__ ____ ____ ____ ____ _____.

Receiver: Could you __4__ _____ ____ _____, please?

Caller: That's E-M-M-A, E-L-I-T-E.

Receiver: Okay, does she have your cell phone number?

Caller: Oh, it's 013-465-8809.

Receiver: All right. Let me __5__ _____ ____ _____. It's zero one three, four six five, __6__ _____ _____ ____ ____.

Caller: Actually, that should be double eight oh nine.

Receiver: I'm sorry about that. All right. I'll __7__ _____ ____ ____ _____.

Caller: Thank you very much. Goodbye.

+ BIZ TIPs 전화 통화, 이것만은 알아두자 ①

▶ **전화번호를 불러줄 때**
전화번호는 보통 한 자리씩 끊어서 읽는다. 숫자 0은 zero라고도 하지만 흔히 oh라고 읽는다. 또, 같은 숫자가 반복되면 숫자 앞에 double을 넣어 읽기도 한다.

9467 – nine four six seven   5048 – five oh four eight
2213 – double two one three

▶ **contact number란?**
contact number라고 하면 당사자와 곧바로 통화할 수 있는 긴급 연락처, 즉 핸드폰 번호(cell phone number)나 직통 번호(direct line)를 뜻한다. 반면, 그냥 telephone number는 home number(자택 전화번호) 등의 모든 전화번호를 통칭하는 말이다.

잘못 걸린 전화와 자동응답기

Wrong Calls and Answering Machine

Vocabulary & Expressions

잘못 걸린 전화 Wrong Number

- **have the wrong number** 전화를 잘못 걸다
- **dial incorrectly** 전화번호를 잘못 누르다
- **Isn't this ...?** ~가 아닌가요?
- **look for** ~를 찾다

자동응답기 Answering Machine

- **leave a message on the answering machine** 자동응답기에 메시지를 남기다
- **miss a call** 전화를 받지 못하다
- **missed call** 부재중 전화
- **new message** 새로운 메시지
- **unplayed message** 듣지 않은 메시지
- **outgoing message** 발신 메시지 (전화 주인이 녹음해 놓는 메시지)
- **incoming message** 수신 메시지 (전화 건 사람이 남겨놓는 메시지)
- **beep** 신호, 삐 소리
- **press + [숫자]** [숫자]를 누르다
- **not be able to take your call** 전화를 받을 수 없다
- **be calling regarding[about]** ~때문에 전화를 걸다
- **reach someone** ~에게 (전화 등으로) 연락하다
- **get back to someone** (전화나 편지로) ~에게 회신 연락하다
- **when you get a chance** 혹시 기회가 있다면

사과에 대한 응답

A: I'm sorry about that.
그 점에 대해 죄송합니다.
I'm so sorry to bother you.
귀찮게 해서 죄송합니다.
B: No worries.
No problem.
Don't sweat it.
Don't worry about it.
괜찮습니다.

메시지를 남긴 후

- listen to one's message 메시지를 듣다
- change one's message 메시지를 수정하다
- delete one's message 메시지를 지우다
- save one's message 메시지를 저장하다

Useful Expressions

What number did you dial?
몇 번으로 전화 거셨나요?

Isn't this 729-4013?
729-4013번 **아닌가요?**

I'm calling regarding the project schedule.
프로젝트 스케줄 **때문에 전화했습니다.**

I'm returning your call.
회신전화 드리는 겁니다.

Who is it that you are looking for?
누구를 찾으시죠?

A Match the meanings on the left with the expressions on the right.

1 전화를 잘못 걸다 · · ⓐ leave a message

2 자동응답기 · · ⓑ have the wrong number

3 메시지를 삭제하다 · · ⓒ delete the message

4 메시지를 남기다 · · ⓓ miss a call

5 전화를 받지 못하다 · · ⓔ answering machine

B Fill in the blanks with the given words.

1 전화를 잘못 거신 것 같습니다.
   ▸ You must _____ _____ the wrong number.

2 잘못된 내선번호로 연결되셨습니다.
   ▸ You've got the _____ _____.

3 거기 사이퍼트레이딩사 아닌가요?
   ▸ _____ _____ the Cyper Trading Company?

4 여기 헨리라는 분은 안 계십니다.
   ▸ _____ _____ no Henry here.

> 📋 Words
> isn't this
> there is
> wrong extension
> have dialed

C Refer to the Korean and fill in the blanks.

1 You've _____ Brenda Lee's phone. 브랜다 리의 전화에 연결되셨습니다. (*자동응답기에 연결됐을 때 나오는 안냇말)

2 _____ _____ did you dial? 몇 번으로 전화 거셨습니까?

3 You've got _____ _____ _____. 전화를 잘못하셨습니다.

4 There's nobody _____ _____ _____ here. 여기 그런 이름을 가진 분은 없는데요.

5 But if you leave a message, I'll _____ _____ to you as soon as I can.
   하지만 메시지를 남겨주시면, 가능한 한 빨리 연락 드리겠습니다.

You've got the wrong number.   전화를 잘못 거셨습니다.

There's nobody with that name here.   여기 그런 이름을 가진 분은 안 계십니다.

No problem. / Don't worry about it. / Don't sweat it.   괜찮습니다.

I'm sorry I'm not available at the moment.   죄송하지만 제가 지금 전화를 받을 수가 없습니다.

If you leave a message, I'll get back to you as soon as I can. 메시지를 남겨주시면 가능한 한 빨리 연락 드리겠습니다.

08.mp3

A Hello? Can I speak to Ms. Clark?

B I'm sorry, but what number did you call?

A ¹**Isn't this** 729-4013?

B ²**Who is it that** you are looking for?

A ³**I'm looking for** someone named Jane Clark.

B I think you've got the wrong number. There's nobody with that name here.

A Sorry about that.

B No worries.

Pattern Training

1 **Isn't this** [＿＿＿＿＿]? ~가 아닌가요?

① LK Electronics
② the Sales Department
③ 010-7855-8314

▶ LK 전자 / 영업부 / 010-7855-8314번

2 **Who is it that** [＿＿＿＿＿]? ~은 누구입니까?

① you wish to speak to
② you are waiting for
③ you are working with

▶ 당신이 통화하길 원하는 분 / 당신이 기다리는 분 / 당신이 함께 일하는 분

3 **I'm looking for** [＿＿＿＿＿]. ~를 찾고 있습니다.

① Ms. Cheryl Burns
② Mr. Harris in the Sales Department
③ someone in charge of accounting

▶ 세릴 번스 씨 / 영업부의 해리스 씨 / 회계 담당자

🔲 전화 대화에서 this

Isn't this …?는 한국어로 하자면 '(거기) ~가 아닌가요?'이다. 그래서 this가 아닌 that을 써야 할 것 같지만, 이때 this는 '내가 한 전화' 즉, 전화를 건 사람 쪽에서 말하는 표현이다. '내가 전화를 건 곳이 OOO 아닌가요?'라는 질문으로 생각하자.

🔲 바른 응답

흔히 저지르는 기본적인 실수 중 하나가 '사과'에 대해 You're welcome.으로 대답하는 것이다. 이 표현은 Thank you.에 대한 대답으로 적절하기 때문이다. 사과하는 말에 대한 대답으로는 No problem., That's okay. 등을 쓰도록 하자.

Leaving a Message to the Answering Machine
자동응답기에 메시지 남기기

09.mp3

Answering Machine

You are trying to reach Lisa's phone. ¹**I am sorry** I'm not able to take your call at the moment, but ²**if you leave a message, I'll** get back to you as soon as I can. Please leave a message after the beep.

Caller

Hello, Ms. Richardson. This is Lawrence Miller. ³**I'm calling regarding** the change of schedule for the monthly meeting that we are having this month. I need to speak to you about it ASAP, so please call me when you get a chance.

Pattern Training

1 **I am sorry** [＿＿＿＿＿＿]. ~해서 죄송합니다.

① I can't answer the phone now
② I didn't get back to you earlier
③ for the inconvenience we have caused

▶ 지금 전화를 받을 수 없어서 / 일찍 연락 드리지 못해서 / 불편을 끼쳐드려서

2 **If you leave a message, I'll** [＿＿＿＿＿＿]. 메시지를 남기시면, ~하겠습니다.

① call you back as soon as I can
② return your call when I can
③ phone you back soon

▶ 가능한 한 빨리 전화하겠습니다 / 가능할 때 전화하겠습니다 / 곧 다시 전화 드리겠습니다

3 **I'm calling regarding** [＿＿＿＿＿＿]. ~때문에 전화했습니다.

① the agenda for the next meeting
② a product I purchased from your store last week
③ the problem we've been facing for the whole year

▶ 다음 회의 안건 / 지난주에 당신 가게에서 구입한 상품 / 우리가 한 해 동안 겪고 있는 문제

A　Find the correct responses to complete the dialogs.

1 What number did you dial?

2 I think you've got the wrong number.

3 Is Soyoung there?

4 I am very sorry.

5 I'm not able to take your call at the moment. Please leave a message after the beep.

Answers

ⓐ There's nobody with that name here.

ⓑ Isn't this 522-2078?

ⓒ I am sorry.

ⓓ That's okay.

ⓔ I'm calling regarding our appointment time.

B　Complete the short dialogs.

1

A: May I speak to Mr. Stanford? This is Jacqueline.

B: Mr. Stanford? _____ ?(몇 번으로 전화 거셨어요?)

A: _____ ?(555–2357번 아닌가요?)

B: I'm sorry, but I think you've got the wrong number.
_____.(여기 그런 이름 가진 분은 없어요.)

2

A: You are trying to reach Jacqueline's phone. I am sorry I'm not able to take your call at the moment, but if you leave a message, I'll get back to you as soon as I can. Please leave a message after the beep.

B: Hi, It's Kevin Stanford, and _____.
(우리의 약속 시간과 관련해서 전화했습니다.) Please _____.
(시간 날 때 전화해 주세요.)

A Listen to the message and check true or false. 10.mp3

	True	False
1 The woman will call again tomorrow.		
2 To change her message, she needs to press the pound key.		
3 To delete her message, she needs to press 3.		

B Listen again and complete the blanks. 10.mp3

Answering machine: You are trying to reach Paul's phone. I am sorry I'm not available at the moment, but if you leave a message, I'll get back to you as soon as I can. Please leave a message after the beep.

Voice message: Hi, Mr. Miller. _1_____ Nancy, Nancy Richardson. I am _2_____ the change of schedule for our meeting. I guess you are not there _3_____. I will try _4_____ later today.

Answering machine: To _5_____ your message, press 1. If you wish to _6_____ your message, press 2. If you wish to _7_____ your message, press 3. Alternatively, press the _8_____ (#) if you wish to _9_____ your message.

+ BIZ TIPs   세련된 문장 만들기

▶ regarding(~에 관해서)은 비즈니스 상황에서 격식을 차린 표현으로 자주 사용된다. regarding, about 뒤에는 명사형 어구가 와야 한다는 점도 명심하자.
I'm calling **regarding** the change of schedule for the monthly meeting.
(월례회의 일정의 변동과 관련해 전화 드렸습니다.)

▶ 어떤 문제점을 설명할 때, 거부감을 줄이기 위해 seem(~인 것 같다) 또는 appear(~처럼 보인다)와 같은 표현을 사용하는 것도 하나의 요령이다.
There seems to be a little problem with the production line. (생산 라인에 약간의 문제가 있는 것 같습니다.)
It appears that we are having a minor glitch with the delivery. (배송에 작은 오류가 있어 보입니다.)

통화 중 문제 발생과 국제전화

Problems with the Phone and International Calls

Vocabulary & Expressions

통화 중 문제 발생 Problems with the Phone

- **bad connection** 연결 상태가 안 좋음
- **low battery** 배터리 부족
- **too noisy** 너무 시끄러운
- **not be working** 전화가 고장 나다 (= be out of order)
- **break up** 말소리가 끊기다
- **hear an echo** 말소리가 울려서 들리다
- **be crossed** 혼선되다
- **be disconnected** 전화 연결이 끊어지다
- **not much credit left** 얼마 남지 않은 전화 사용 한도액
- **pre-paid phone** 선불전화 (= pay-as-you-go)

국제전화 International Calls

- **time difference** 시차
- **country code** 국가 번호
- **area code** 지역 번호
- **international dialing prefix** 국제전화용 코드(번호)
- **ahead of** (시간상) ~보다 앞선
- **behind** (시간상) ~보다 늦은
- **be [시간] behind** [시간]만큼 뒤지다

📞 통화가 곤란한 상황

- have a meeting to attend
  참석해야 할 회의가 있다
- be swamped with
  ~에 파묻혀 있다, ~일로 바쁘다
- have a visitor
  손님이 있다
- call back
  (전화를 한 사람에게) 다시 전화하다
- talk to you another time
  다른 시간에 통화하다

Useful Expressions

The connection is not so good.	연결 상태가 별로 좋지 않습니다.
You are breaking up.	말소리가 끊겨서 들려요.
I couldn't get through because the line was busy.	통화 중이라서 전화 연결이 안 됐어요.
My battery is almost dead.	배터리가 거의 다 되었어요.
My phone is not working.	전화기가 고장 났습니다.

A Match the meanings on the left with the expressions on the right.

1 선불전화 ·   · ⓐ have a visitor

2 손님이 있다 ·   · ⓑ break up

3 통화 소리가 끊기다 ·   · ⓒ bad connection

4 연결상태가 좋지 않음 ·   · ⓓ pre-paid phone

5 소리가 울린다 ·   · ⓔ hear an echo

B Fill in the blanks with the given words.

1 전화 소리가 끊겨요.
  ▸ You are _____ _____.

2 통화 중이었어요.
  ▸ The line was _____.

3 배터리가 거의 다 되었어요.
  ▸ My battery is almost _____.

4 제 전화기가 고장 났어요.
  ▸ My phone is not _____.

🔵 Words

busy
break up
dead
work

C Refer to the Korean and fill in the blanks.

1 What is the _____ _____ for Malaysia? 말레이시아의 국가 번호가 몇 번이죠?

2 You need to check the _____ _____ between Seoul and L.A. so that you don't wake your client up in the middle of the night. 한밤중에 고객을 깨우지 않으려면 서울과 L.A. 간의 시차를 확인해야 합니다.

3 Where can I get an _____ _____ _____? 국제전화카드는 어디서 살 수 있습니까?

4 How many hours is Washington _____ Seoul? 워싱턴은 서울보다 몇 시간 느린가요?

5 Is Seoul 16 hours _____ _____ Calgary? 서울이 캘거리보다 16시간 빠른가요?

My credit is almost used up.   통화 사용 한도가 얼마 남지 않았습니다.

Can I talk to you another time?   나중에 통화해도 될까요?

I can't really talk to you as I have a meeting to attend soon.   제가 곧 회의에 참석해야 해서 통화할 수 없습니다.

Can I call you back later?   나중에 전화 드려도 될까요?

London is 8 hours behind during the daylight saving period.   런던은 서머타임 기간 동안 8시간이 늦습니다.

11.mp3

A ¹**You are breaking up, so** I can only partially hear you.

B Pardon?

A It's a very bad connection. I can hear an echo, so I can hardly hear you.

B Really? It's all right on my side. Well, let me call you again.

A My battery is almost dead. ²**Shall we continue this talk** another time?

B Sure. When can you call me again?

A I'm busy until Thursday. Why don't you call me after Thursday?

B Great. I'll call you at 10 a.m. on Friday morning.

Pattern Training

1   **You are breaking up, so** [_____]. 말소리가 끊겨서 ~.

① I can barely hear you
② I think I should talk to you later
③ I'm not sure what you are saying

▶ 당신의 말이 거의 들리질 않습니다 / 나중에 얘기해야겠습니다 / 무슨 말인지 모르겠어요

2   **Shall we continue this talk** [_____]? 이 이야기를 ~ 계속할까요?

① tomorrow
② by e-mail
③ in my office

▶ 내일 / 이메일로 / 제 사무실에서

12.mp3

A Linda, **¹I'd like to** ask you a few things about how to make international calls.

B Sure, go ahead.

A I'd like to call Paul in Rome and what time is it there now?

B It's five thirty a.m. in Rome now.

A Then could you connect the call in 4 hours?

B Yes, **²I'll connect you to** Paul in four hours.

A Ah, **³please tell me how much** the phone call is per minute as well.

B Yes, it's 1,045(one thousand forty five) won per minute.

Pattern Training \

1 I'd like to ⌐‒‒‒‒‒‒‒‒‒‒‒¬. ~하고 싶습니다.

① place a collect call to London
② get an international calling card
③ sign up for the international calling service

▶ 런던으로 수신자 부담 전화를 걸고 / 국제전화카드를 사고 / 국제전화서비스에 가입하고

2 I'll connect you to ⌐‒‒‒‒‒‒‒‒‒‒‒¬. 전화를 ~에게 연결해 드리겠습니다.

① someone who speaks German
② the International Cooperation Division
③ a customer service representative

▶ 독일어를 하시는 분께 / 국제 협력팀으로 / 고객서비스 담당자에게

3 Please tell me how much ⌐‒‒‒‒‒‒‒‒‒‒‒¬. ~가 얼마인지 말씀해 주세요.

① this international calling card is
② your international calling plan is per minute
③ that will be

▶ 이 국제전화카드 / 분당 국제전화 요금제 / 예상되는 비용

A   Find the correct responses to complete the dialogs.

1   Oh, Mr. Jackson. I've been waiting for your call all morning.

2   Hey, can you call me back? My credit is almost used up on my cell.

3   Could I… Mr. Ro… son… Is he…?

4   Hi. How's it going? I haven't heard from you for ages.

5   I'm sorry, but I can't really talk to you at the moment. I have a meeting to attend in a moment.

6   I'm afraid it's not a good time for me to talk. I have some clients here with me.

> **Answers**
> ⓐ My cell phone has not been working for a while. I just got a new cell phone now.
> ⓑ Sorry, but your line has been busy all morning. That's why I'm returning your call now.
> ⓒ Okay. Could you call me once you are alone?
> ⓓ Your credit is low? Sure, I'll call right back.
> ⓔ Sorry? You are breaking up.
> ⓕ Oh, then I'd better let you go now. Please give me a call after the meeting.

B   Complete the short dialogs.

1

A: Excuse me, Yeonsoo. Do you know how many hours Budapest is behind or ahead of Seoul?

B: Budapest? I think _____.(서울보다 7시간 늦는 것 같아요.) Because of daylight saving time. It would normally have been 8 hours behind if it weren't for that.

A: So that means _____, right?
(그 말은 서울이 부다페스트보다 7시간 빠르다는 뜻이에요?)

B: I guess so.

2

A: Hello, Mr. Johnson. This is Jim Stevens calling.

B: I'm sorry, but I can't _____.
(뭐라고 말씀하시는지 안 들려요.) We have _____.
(전화 연결 상태가 안 좋아요.)

A: _____.(그럼 제가 더 크게 말해 볼게요.) I said that it's Jim Stevens.

B: Jim who? I'm sorry, but I still can't hear you. Why don't you _____ _____?(전화를 끊고 다시 거는 게 어때요?)

A　Listen to the dialog and answer the questions.

13.mp3

1 What is the caller's name?
▶ _____

2 Which company does the woman work for?
▶ _____

3 What was the reason the woman returned the man call so late?
▶ _____

B　Listen again and complete the blanks.

13.mp3

Jessica:　Hello. Could I __¹_____ _____ Mr. Scott, please?

Mr. Scott:　__²_____ .

Jessica:　Hello, Mr. Scott. __³_____ is Jessica Norman _____ Connections Telecom.
I believe you __⁴_____ _____ _____ on my answering machine?

Mr. Scott:　Hello, Ms. Norman. I have been __⁵_____ _____ your call.

Jessica:　I'm sorry for __⁶_____ _____ ____ _____ . Actually, I've just returned from a
business trip.

Mr. Scott:　That explains it. I didn't know about that.

C　Listen to the dialog and check true or false.

14.mp3

1 The company's name is TTS.　[T] [F]

2 The person who accepts the collect call is Mr. Peter Jackson.　[T] [F]

3 The receiver wants to accept the collect call.　[T] [F]

+ BIZ TIPs　전화 통화, 이것만은 알아두자 ②

▶ **My phone is out of order?**
핸드폰이 고장 났을 때 be out of order라는 표현을 활용해서 My phone is out of order.라고 말하면 될 것 같지만 사실 이 표현은 주로 복사기나 기계류, 공중전화와 같은 큰 기기에 사용하는 표현이다. be out of order보다는 My phone is not working.이란 표현이 더 일반적인 표현이라는 것을 기억하면서, 핸드폰이 고장 났을 때 한번 활용해 보자.

▶ **서머타임(daylight saving time 일광절약시간제)**
북미와 유럽의 많은 국가는 여름 동안 시간을 한 시간 앞당겨 맞춰서 일광 시간을 활용해 전기를 아끼는 서머타임을 시행하고 있다. 미국 대부분 지역은 3월 둘째 주 일요일 새벽 2시에 서머타임을 시작해서 11월 첫째 주 일요일에 원래 시간으로 되돌린다. 따라서 국제전화를 걸 때 한국과의 시차 계산 시 참고하면 아직 단잠을 자고 있는 사람을 깨우는 등의 실수를 줄일 수 있을 것이다.

Walt Disney
"The Pioneer of the Motion Picture Industry"

Walt Disney, the founder of Walt Disney Studios, Disney World, and Disneyland Park, started by tasting [1] **the first bitter fruits of life**. After his company, Laugh-O-Grams, [2] **went bankrupt**, he headed to Hollywood with one suitcase and twenty dollars in his pocket.

People began to recognize him after he [3] **made a success of** of his *Alice Comedies,* and then he won the first of his studio's Academy Awards in 1932 with *Flowers and Trees,* which was the very first cartoon in color. In 1937, he released the first short subject to utilize the multi-plane camera technique, *The Old Mill,* followed by *Snow White and the Seven Dwarfs*, the first full-length animated musical feature.

Although it cost him $1,499,000 during the depths of the Depression, he [4] **was** very **satisfied with** the film as the film is loved by everyone, and it is still considered one of the greatest feats and imperishable monuments of the motion picture industry. Walt Disney Studios continued to produce other full-length animated classics, such as *Pinocchio*, *Fantasia*, *Dumbo*, and *Bambi* for the next five year after *Snow White and the Seven Dwarfs*. He pursued his dream, Disneyland Park, which opened in 1955.

Walt Disney is a man who taught us and showed us that dreams can [5] **come true** if you work hard enough. He is a legend and a hero to many of us and will continue to be in our hearts forever.

월트 디즈니 ― "영화 산업의 선구자"

월트 디즈니 스튜디오와 디즈니 월드, 디즈니랜드의 창설자인 월트 디즈니는 인생에 있어 첫 쓴맛을 보며 시작했다. 자신의 회사인 Laugh-O-Grams가 파산하자 그는 여행가방 하나와 달랑 20달러만 주머니에 넣은 채 할리우드로 향했다.

그가 '앨리스 코미디'로 성공하자 사람들이 인정하기 시작했고, 그 후 1932년에 최초의 컬러 만화인 '꽃과 나무'로 그의 스튜디오는 아카데미상을 수상했다. 1937년에는 최초의 장편 뮤지컬 애니메이션인 '백설공주와 일곱 난쟁이들'에 이어 멀티플레인 카메라 기술을 이용한 첫 단편영화인 '올드 밀'을 출시하였다.

그는 격심한 대공황의 시기에 1,499,000달러의 비용을 들여가면서도 사람들에게 사랑받는 영화를 만드는 것에 흡족해했으며, 그의 영화는 지금까지도 영화 산업에서 위대한 업적이자 기념비적 작품 중 하나로 인정받고 있다. 월트 디즈니 스튜디오는 '백설공주와 일곱 난쟁이들' 이후 5년 동안 계속해서 '피노키오', '환타지아', '덤보', '밤비'와 같은 클래식 장편 애니메이션들을 제작하였다. 1955년에는 그는 자신의 꿈이 투영된 디즈니랜드 테마공원을 개장하였다.

월트 디즈니는 우리에게 열심히 하면 꿈이 실현된다는 것을 가르쳐주고 보여주었다. 그는 전설이며 대중의 영웅으로서 영원히 우리들의 가슴 속에 간직될 것이다.

1 taste the first bitter fruits of life 인생의 첫 쓴맛을 보다

▶ 힘들고 어려웠다는 것을 은유적으로 표현한 것, '어떤 일의 흡족하지 않은 결과'를 의미하기도 한다.

The unemployed are **tasting the bitter fruits** of the market economy.

실업자들은 시장 경제의 쓴맛을 보고 있다.

2 go bankrupt 파산하다, 돈이 없는 상태다

The recession has led to many small businesses **going bankrupt**.

불황으로 인해 많은 소기업이 파산하였다.

3 make a success of ~에 성공하다

▶ 이와 반대로 make a mess of는 '~에 실패하다'란 의미

He has **made a big success of** movies.

그는 영화로 큰 성공을 거두었다.

4 be satisfied with ~에 만족하다

Are you **satisfied with** the new arrangement?

새로운 결정에 만족합니까?

5 come true 실현되다, 현실화되다

I hope all my resolutions will **come true** this year.

올해에는 내 결심들이 모두 실현되었으면 좋겠다.

Disneyland Park

Who is Walt Disney?

월트 디즈니 스튜디오와 디즈니 월드, 디즈니랜드 테마파크의 창설자인 월트 디즈니는 영화 감독, 프로듀서, 극작가, 애니메이션 작가, 기업가로, 열심히 노력하면 꿈을 실현할 수 있다는 것을 보여준 인물이다. 미키 마우스 등 세계적인 만화영화 캐릭터를 창조해내어 많은 사랑을 받았으며, 1930년대 만화영화 부문의 상을 독점하다시피 하여 무려 64번이나 아카데미상에 노미네이트된 기록을 보유하고 있다.

Walt Disney says...

"The way to get started is to quit talking and begin doing."

시작하는 방법은 말하길 멈추고 행동하는 것이다.

"The era we are living in today is a dream of coming true."

우리가 현재 살고 있는 이 시대가 꿈의 실현입니다.

"When we consider a project, we really study it— not just the surface idea, but everything about it. And when we go into that new project, we believe in it all the way. We have confidence in our ability to do it right. And we work hard to do the best possible job."

프로젝트를 생각할 때, 우리는 그것에 대해 단편적인 아이디어뿐만 아니라 모든 것을 연구합니다. 그리고 새로운 프로젝트에 착수할 때, 언제나 그것에 대한 믿음을 가집니다. 우리는 그 일을 올바르게 수행할 능력이 있음을 자신합니다. 그리고 가능한 한 최고의 일을 해내고자 노력합니다.

General Business
Daily Routines at the Office

PART 2

사무실에서의 일상 업무

WEEK 04

미팅 약속 정하기

Making an Arrangement for Meeting

Vocabulary & Expressions

약속 정하기 Setting up an Appointment

- **set up an appointment** 약속을 정하다 (set up = make, arrange)
- **check the schedule** 일정을 확인하다
- **be scheduled to** ~하기로 되어 있다 (= be arranged to, be supposed to)
- **set a date** 날짜를 정하다
- **make it** 약속을 지키다 (not to make it 약속을 못 지키다)
- **day-planner** 스케줄러, 다이어리
- **prior engagement** 선약

📅 약속 날짜 정하기 [on+월+날짜]
- I'm available to see you on March 2.
  3월 2일에 만나뵐 수 있어요.

📅 약속 시간 정하기 [at+시간]
- I'd like to see you at 11:40 a.m.
  오전 11시 40분에 뵙고 싶습니다.

약속 취소하기 Canceling an Appointment

- **cancel** 취소하다
- **postpone** 연기하다 (= put off)
- **take a rain-check** 다음으로 미루다, 연기하다
- **reschedule** 일정을 다시 잡다 (= rearrange)
- **confirm an appointment** 약속을 확인하다
- **make it earlier** 약속을 앞당기다
- **make it later** 약속을 늦추다
- **be tied up** ~에 묶이다, 매우 바쁘다
- **be running late** 지체되고 있다
- **be held up** (교통 체증 등으로) 꼼짝 못 하다

> I think I'll have to **take a rain-check**.
> I forgot about a prior engagement.
> 다음 기회로 미뤄야 할 것 같습니다. 선약이 있는 걸 깜빡 잊었어요.

Useful Expressions

Let's make an appointment .	약속을 정합시다.
I'm sorry, but I can't make it that day.	죄송하지만 그날은 **약속을 잡을 수 없습니다.**
I have a prior engagement.	선약이 있습니다.
I'm afraid we need to reschedule our meeting.	미팅 시간을 다시 잡아야 할 것 같습니다.
Some important thing has just come up.	갑자기 중요한 일이 생겼어요.

Vocabulary Check-Up

A Match the meanings on the left with the expressions on the right.

1 약속을 정하다 ·   · ⓐ day-planner

2 선약이 있다 ·   · ⓑ reschedule the meeting

3 약속을 앞당기다 ·   · ⓒ have a prior engagement

4 스케줄러 ·   · ⓓ set up an appointment

5 회의 일정을 다시 잡다 ·   · ⓔ make it earlier

B Fill in the blanks with the given words.

1 다음 기회로 미뤄도 될까요?

   ▶ Can I take _____ _____?

2 차가 막혀서 발이 묶였어요.

   ▶ I _____ _____ _____ in traffic.

3 수요일은 좀 바빠서 약속을 못 지킬 것 같습니다.

   ▶ I am a bit _____ _____ on Wednesday, so I don't think I can make it.

4 그날은 제가 시간이 안 됩니다.

   ▶ I'm not _____ on that day.

> **Words**
> a rain-check
> available
> be held up
> tied up

C Refer to the Korean and fill in the blanks.

1 I'm afraid something else _____ _____, so I can't _____ _____ today.

   다른 일이 생겨서 오늘 약속을 못 지킬 것 같습니다.

2 Shall we _____ _____ _____ for our next meeting now? 다음 미팅 날짜를 지금 정할까요?

3 Why don't we _____ _____ a little _____? 약속 시간을 조금 늦추는 게 어때요?

4 I know I _____ _____ _____ visit your office this Saturday, but I don't think I can make it.

   이번 주 토요일에 당신 사무실을 방문하기로 되어 있었는데, 약속을 못 지킬 것 같아요.

5 When would be a _____ _____? 언제 시간이 좋으신가요?

What day would be good for you?   며칠이 좋으세요?

How about next Monday at 2 p.m.?   다음 주 월요일 오후 2시가 **어떠세요**?

I'm sorry, but I'm going to have to cancel tomorrow's lunch.   **죄송하지만**, 내일 점심 **약속을 취소해야겠네요**.

Can I postpone it to another time?   **다른 시간으로 미뤄도 될까요?**

I'm sorry, but I'm running a little late.   미안하지만 **좀 늦을 것 같아요.**

15.mp3

A Hello? May I speak to Mr. Thomas? This is Jane from the ICN Corporation.

B Jane, hi! How are you doing?

A Not bad, Mr. Thomas. [1]**I'd like to** set a date for our next meeting. What day would be good for you?

B [2]**How about** Wednesday at around 2 p.m.?

A [3]**Let me** check my schedule first **before** we can make any sort of arrangement.

B Okay, I will hold.

A I'm sorry, but I can't make it that day. How about Friday instead?

B Sure. That would be fine with me. Then I'll see you on Friday.

Pattern Training

1   **I'd like to** _____. ~하고 싶습니다.

① make an appointment
② postpone it until another time
③ talk to you about the appointment

▶ 약속을 잡고 / 약속을 다른 때로 연기하고 / 약속에 관해 이야기하고

🔲 편한 약속 시간 묻기
- What day would be good for you?
- When would be a good time?
- What time would you like?
- When are you free?
  언제가 좋으세요?

2   **How about** _____? ~가 어떠세요?

① next Monday at 2 p.m.
② Friday afternoon
③ tomorrow instead

▶ 다음 주 월요일 오후 2시 / 금요일 오후 / 대신에 내일

3   **Let me** _____ **before** _____. ~하기 전에, …할게요.

① speak to you, I set off
② get a coffee, I get to work
③ book a flight, I plan anything else for this trip

▶ 출발하기 전에, 당신에게 말할게요 / 일을 시작하기 전에, 커피를 마실게요 / 여행 계획을 짜기 전에, 비행기를 예약할게요

16.mp3

A Hello, David speaking.

B Hi, this is Jane. I know we were supposed to have a few drinks on Friday, but [1]**I'm going to have to** cancel our appointment. Can we reschedule it?

A Sure. Just [2]**let me know** when you want to do it.

B How about next Monday at the same time? [3]**What's** your schedule **like**?

A Oh, sure. Monday is fine with me. Well, see you later then.

Pattern Training

1 **I'm going to have to** [_____]. ~해야 합니다.

① work on our proposal this week
② go on a business trip
③ reschedule our meeting

▶ 이번 주에 우리의 계획을 추진해야 / 출장을 가야 / 우리의 미팅 일정을 조정해야

2 **Let me know** [_____]. ~를 알려 주세요.

① when you have time
② when you can make it
③ when we can meet

▶ 언제 시간이 나는지 / 언제 약속이 가능한지 / 언제 만날 수 있는지

3 **What's** [_____] **like?** (상태·외모·성격 등)은 어떤가요?

① he
② the weather
③ the meeting

▶ 그분 / 날씨 / 미팅(회의)

A Fill in the blanks with the given words.

when	schedule	make	how	with
earlier	set	afraid	convenient	like

1 A: Shall we _____ a date for our next meeting now?

   B: Sure, _____ are you free?

   지금 다음 미팅 날짜를 정할까요? – 그러죠. 언제 시간 되세요?

2 A: What's the most _____ time for you?

   B: Oh, any day is fine _____ me.

   언제가 가장 편하세요? – 아무 때나 저는 좋아요.

3 A: I'm _____ something else came up. Can you _____ it a little _____?

   B: Sure! I can come over at 11.

   유감스럽게도 갑자기 일이 생겼어요. 약속 시간을 좀 당겨도 될까요? – 그러죠! 11시까지 갈 수 있습니다.

4 A: I'm sorry, but tomorrow is a busy day for me.

   B: _____ about Friday then? What's your _____ _____?

   죄송하지만 내일은 바쁜 날이에요. – 그럼 금요일은 어때요? 스케줄이 되시나요?

B Complete the short dialogs.

A: Hello, This is Daniel Reed speaking.

B: Hi, this is Sarah. I'm afraid to say __1_____
_____.(월요일 약속을 지킬 수 없겠어요.) __2_____
_____?(약속 일정을 다시 잡을 수 있을까요?)

A: Sure, how about Thursday?

B: Just a second. __3_____.(먼저 제 일정을 확인해 볼게요.)
Oh, __4_____.(목요일은 괜찮네요.)

A: Okay, how about at 2 o'clock?

B: Oh, sure. I'll see you on Thursday at 2 o'clock.

+ BIZ TIPs   약속 내용을 변경할 때는 change가 아니라 reschedule

미팅 일정을 다시 잡을 때 change our meeting이라고 표현하는 것을 자주 보는데, 이는 '미팅을 바꾸다'라는 말이 되어 어색하게 들릴 수 있다. 영어적 시각에서 봤을 때는 미팅을 바꾸는 것이 아니라 미팅 일정을 다시 잡는 것이므로 reschedule our meeting이라고 말해야 훨씬 자연스러운 표현이다. 단, 미팅의 세부적인 사항인 날짜나 시간, 장소 등을 바꾸는 것은 change로 표현할 수 있다.

A Listen to the dialog and check true or false.

17.mp3

	True	False
1 The man wants to talk about a new project.		
2 Thursday is a busy day for the man.		
3 The two of them are going to meet on Friday.		

B Listen again and complete the blanks.

17.mp3

Mark: Hello, this is Mark Sanders speaking. ¹_____ ____ _____ _____ Julie Simpson?

Julie: ²_____ ____ Julie. What can I do for you, Mark?

Mark: I would really like to ³_____ ____ _____ _____ _____ to talk to you about our new project. ⁴_____ ____ _____ to get together this Thursday morning?

Julie: I'm sorry, but Thursday ⁵_____ _____ ____ ____. I'll be ⁶_____ ____ _____ _____ all day. How about Friday afternoon instead?

Mark: Okay, I can do that. Is four o'clock an acceptable time?

Julie: It sounds perfect. ⁷_____ _____ _____ ____ seeing you.

C Listen to the dialog and answer the questions.

18.mp3

1 Why does the man make the phone call?

▶ _____

2 Why does the man have to reschedule their meeting?

▶ _____

3 When are the two going to meet?

▶ _____

WEEK 05
출퇴근 인사와 휴가 신청

Greeting at Work and Asking for Leave

Vocabulary & Expressions

사무실에서의 하루 A Day at the Office

- **go to work / get to work** 출근하다
- **be late for** ~에 지각하다
- **have a coffee break** 커피 마시며 쉬다
- **go out for lunch** 점심식사 하러 나가다
- **wrap up** (일·회의 등을) 끝마치다
- **leave the office** 퇴근하다
- **call it a day** 일과를 마치다

조퇴/휴가 신청하기 Asking for Leave

- **take a day off** 하루 쉬다, 하루 휴가를 내다
- **leave early** 조퇴하다 (= take off early)
- **cover for someone** ~의 빈자리를 채워주다, ~ 대신 일하다
- **be fed up with** ~에 진절머리가 나다 (= sick and tired of)
- **work around the clock** 24시간 내내 일하다, 매우 열심히 일하다
- **call in sick** 전화로 병가를 내다, 아파서 전화하다
- **work overtime** 야근하다
- **feel under the weather** 몸이 안 좋다

지각 사유 말하기

- **My alarm clock didn't go off this morning.**
  알람 시계가 오늘 아침에 안 울렸어요.
- **The subway was just packed.**
  지하철이 만원이었어요.
- **I overslept this morning.**
  아침에 늦잠을 잤습니다.
- **I was stuck in a traffic jam for an hour.**
  한 시간 동안 교통체증에 갇혀 있었어요.

휴가의 종류

- **leave** (신청에 따른) 휴가
  vacation 정기 휴가, (여행 등의) 휴가
  holiday 휴일, 휴가
- **monthly leave** 월차
  annual leave 연차
  paid leave 유급 휴가
  a week's holiday 주간 휴일
  summer holiday 여름 휴가
  maternity leave 출산 휴가

Useful Expressions

I leave my office at 6 o'clock.	저는 6시에 **퇴근합니다.**
May I leave early?	**조퇴해도** 될까요?
Shall we call it a day?	그만 마칠까요?
I'd like to take tomorrow off.	내일 **쉬었으면** 합니다.
I had to call in sick.	전화로 **병가를** 내야 했습니다.

A Match the meanings on the left with the expressions on the right.

1 늦잠 자다 · · ⓐ monthly leave
2 ~에 지각하다 · · ⓑ be late for
3 출근하다 · · ⓒ maternity leave
4 월차 · · ⓓ oversleep
5 출산 휴가 · · ⓔ go to work

B Fill in the blanks with the given words.

1 조퇴해도 될까요?
▶ Can I _____ _____ early?

2 출근하는 데 얼마나 걸려요?
▶ How long does it take to _____ _____ _____?

3 병에 걸린 것 같아요.
▶ I think I'm _____ _____ with something.

4 교통체증으로 꼼짝 못 했어요. 다시는 늦지 않겠습니다.
▶ I _____ _____ _____ traffic. I won't be _____ again.

Words
be stuck in
take off
late
get to work
come down

C Refer to the Korean and fill in the blanks.

1 I need to take _____ _____. 내일 휴가를 내야 합니다.
2 I had to _____ _____ _____ because my cold is getting worse. 감기가 점점 심해져서 전화로 병가를 내야 했습니다.
3 I'm thinking of leaving early. Do you think you can _____ _____ me?
조퇴해야 할 것 같은데, 저 대신 일해 줄 수 있나요?
4 Let's _____ it _____ _____ and go out for a drink. 자, 오늘 일은 여기서 마치고 한잔하러 갑시다.
5 I took Monday off as an _____ _____ day. 연차로 월요일을 쉬었어요.

I think I'm coming down with something. 병에 걸린 것 같아요.
I'm a little under the weather . 몸이 좀 안 좋아요.
Mr. Wilson will cover for me . 윌슨 씨가 저를 대신할 겁니다.
I need to work overtime again today. 오늘도 야근해야 합니다.
Take it easy. 쉬엄쉬엄하세요.

19.mp3

A Good morning, Janet! How's it going?

B Morning, very well. You?

A Actually I'm so tired. I got just over 3 hours of sleep last night.

B Why is that?

A I have worked overtime 4 days in a row on the new project.

B That's too bad. But take care of yourself first.

A [1]**I wish I could** take a day off.

B When do you think you're going to finish?

A I'm not sure, but [2]**it'll probably take** another week to complete.

Pattern Training

1 **I wish I could** :_____:.

~하면 좋을 텐데.

① leave earlier than five o'clock
② take a week off
③ call in sick today

▶ 5시 이전에 조퇴할 수 있다면 / 일주일 휴가를 낼 수 있다면 / 오늘 병가를 낼 수 있다면

2 **It'll probably take** :_____:.

아마도 (시간)이 걸릴 겁니다.

① an hour just to get there
② a day to fix the problem
③ three hours to finish editing these reports

▶ 거기 도착하는 데 한 시간이 / 문제를 해결하는 데 하루가 / 이 보고서의 편집을 끝마치는 데 세 시간이

🔊 가벼운 안부 인사와 답변 표현

Q: How's it going?
= How are you doing?
= How have you been?
= How's everything?
= What's up?

A: Very well. You?
= Not too bad. What about you?
= I'm doing great. How about you?
= Great. And you?

* 아침 출근 인사로는 Good morning! 또는 Morning!이 가장 일반적이다.

20.mp3

A Hello. Mr. Walker, It's Jane. I'm calling to tell you that I can't come in today.

B **¹Do you care to explain why** you are calling in sick?

A Because I've been as sick as a dog all night. So I couldn't even open my eyes when I woke up.

B I've heard that you haven't been well lately. I hope you will be over the hump soon.

A Thank you, sir. **²I'm sure I'll** be better by tomorrow. I just need some rest.

B By the way, **³are you done with** your work for the meeting tomorrow?

A Almost. Paul is going to cover for me.

B Okay. Take good care of yourself.

Pattern Training

1 **Do you care to explain why** [＿＿＿＿＿＿＿]? ~한 이유를 설명해 주시겠어요?

① you are late
② you did what you did
③ you are going that way

▶ 당신이 늦은 이유를 / 왜 그랬는지를 / 왜 그러는지를

2 **I'm sure I'll** [＿＿＿＿＿＿＿]. 제가 ~할 거라고 확신합니다.

① do a good job
② be a valuable asset to your company
③ succeed

▶ 잘 해낼 것이라고 / 당신의 회사에 귀중한 자산이 될 것이라고 / 성공할 것이라고

3 **Are you done with** [＿＿＿＿＿＿＿]? ~을 마쳤습니까?

① the report
② your dinner
③ the newspaper

▶ 보고서 / 저녁식사 / 신문 (신문 읽기를)

A   Find the correct responses to complete the dialogs.

1   Good morning, John. How's it going?

2   You don't look good. What's wrong?

3   Shall we call it a day?

4   I'm leaving now. Have a good one.

5   How was your weekend?

> **Answers**
> ⓐ Certainly. We can continue this tomorrow.
> ⓑ I'm a little under the weather.
> ⓒ Yeah, you too. Catch you tomorrow.
> ⓓ Morning. Very well. You?
> ⓔ Not bad. It was a quiet weekend.

B   Complete the short dialog.

A: Hello. Mr. Allen, it's Johnny. I'm calling ___1_____

_____.(오늘 회사에 나갈 수가 없어서 전화했어요.)

B: Do you care to explain ___2_____?

(전화로 병가를 내는 이유를 말해 주겠어요?)

A: My lower back has been giving me some trouble lately. Today it has gotten worse.

B: That's too bad. You'd better see a doctor. And ___3_____

_____.(그리고 며칠 푹 쉬어요.)

A: Thank you, sir. I'm sure ___4_____.

(곧 좋아질 거예요.)

A Listen to the dialog and answer the questions.   21.mp3

1 Why was the woman not in the office for a while?

▶ _____

2 What happened at the office while the woman was gone?

▶ _____

3 What happened to her boss?

▶ _____

B Listen again and complete the blanks.   21.mp3

Kevin: Hey, welcome back to the office. How _¹_____ _____ _____ _____ _____?

Linda: It was really relaxing. It felt so good to be able to _²_____ _____ _____ _____

_____ ____ _____.

Kevin: That must have been nice.

Linda: So _³_____ _____ _____ ____?

Kevin: I've been great. _⁴_____ ____ _____ _____ ____. Ah, while you were

gone, you missed a lot of exciting things.

Linda: Really? What happened while I was away? _⁵_____ _____ _____ _____?

Kevin: No, no one got fired. However, they posted a list of people _⁶_____ _____ on the

bulletin board. _⁷_____ _____ _____ _____ _____.

C Listen to the dialog and check true or false.   22.mp3

	True	False
1 The man has been working overtime a lot.		
2 The man is getting sick.		
3 The man doesn't have to finish his report before lunch.		

감사와 격려 표현하기

Expressing Appreciation and Encouragement

Vocabulary & Expressions

감사와 축하 Appreciation & Congratulations

- **Thank you for -ing** ~해 주셔서 감사합니다
- **appreciate** 고마워하다
- **congratulate someone on** ~에 대해 …을 축하하다
- **value / treasure / cherish** 가치를 존중하다, 소중히 하다
- **feel pleased with** ~에 기뻐하다

격려와 위로 Encouragement & Commiserating

- **I'm sorry to ...** ~해서 유감입니다.
- **commiserate with** ~을 위로하다
- **express one's sorrow for** ~에 대해 애도를 표하다
- **express one's condolences to** ~에게 조의를 표하다
- **feel compassion for** ~에 동정심을 느끼다, 측은한 마음을 가지다
- **sympathize with** ~을 동정하다 (= have sympathy for)
- **regret** 유감스럽게 생각하다

🗨 축하 이벤트
- **birthday** 생일
- **wedding anniversary** 결혼기념일
- **promotion** 승진
- **a big success** 큰 성공
- **a foundation day** 창립일
- **giving birth** 출산

🗨 격려 표현
- **Cheer up!**
  기운 내요!
- **There will be a light at the end of the tunnel.**
  고난 끝에 밝은 날이 올 겁니다.
- **Don't let it get to you!**
  신경 쓰지 마세요!
- **You will succeed if you stick with it to the bitter end.**
  당신이 끝까지 버텨낸다면 성공할 것입니다.
- **Be confident in yourself.**
  자신감을 가지세요.

🗨 칭찬 표현
- **That's great.** 훌륭하군요.
- **You have done well.** 잘하셨습니다.
- **You did a good job.** 훌륭히 해내셨군요.
- **I'm very proud of you.** 당신이 무척 자랑스럽습니다.

Useful Expressions

Thank you for the gift.	선물 **감사합니다.**
I appreciate it.	**(그것에 대해) 감사드립니다.**
Congratulations on your new job.	새로운 직장을 얻으신 것 **축하합니다.**
I owe you one.	(도움에 대해) **고마워요.** [신세 졌어요.]
I value your opinion.	당신의 의견을 **높이 삽니다.**

A Match the meanings on the left with the expressions on the right.

1 승진 · · ⓐ a foundation day

2 실직 · · ⓑ appreciate

3 창립일 · · ⓒ express one's sorrow

4 애도를 표하다 · · ⓓ promotion

5 감사히 여기다 · · ⓔ losing a job

B Fill in the blanks with the given words.

1 정보를 주셔서 감사합니다. 큰 도움이 될 겁니다.

▶ I _____ your input. It will be a great help.

2 어떤 기분인지는 알지만 기운 내세요!

▶ I know how you feel, but _____ _____!

3 가족에 대한 안 좋은 소식을 듣게 되어 유감입니다.

▶ I _____ _____ the terrible news about your family.

4 깊은 조의를 표합니다.

▶ We would like to _____ _____ _____ to you.

Words
express one's condolences
regret
appreciate
cheer up
hear

C Refer to the Korean and fill in the blanks.

1 I'm _____ to hear that. 유감이네요.

2 You will succeed if you _____ _____ _____ to the bitter end. 당신이 끝까지 버텨낸다면 성공할 겁니다.

3 Thanks. That _____ a lot to me. 고마워요. 제게 큰 위로가 됩니다.

4 _____ on your promotion. 승진 축하드립니다.

5 I fully _____ your feelings. 당신의 기분을 잘 이해합니다.

I am sorry to hear that. / I am sorry for you.	유감입니다.
What a pity. / That's a pity.	애석한 일이군요.
I regreted hearing that your father has passed away.	아버님이 돌아가셨다는 소식을 듣게 되어 유감입니다.
My condolences to you and your family.	당신을 비롯해 가족분들께 조의를 표합니다.
It means a lot.	큰 위로가 됩니다.

23.mp3

A Hello, Mr. Parker. Thank you for coming.

B ¹**Thank you for** inviting me. This is for you.

A Ah, you didn't have to bring anything. Hey, it's wine. I love wine. Well, thank you.

B Oh, don't mention it. It's really not much, but I thought you might like something like this.

A Oh, I've heard about the good news. ²**Congratulations on** your promotion.

B ³**I appreciate** that.

A So what is your new title now?

B I believe it's Managing Director.

Pattern Training

1 **Thank you for** _____.

~해서 고맙습니다.

① your hospitality
② your advice
③ your help

▶ 환대해 주셔서 / 충고해 주셔서 / 도와주셔서

🔵 도움에 대한 감사 표현

Thank you for all the help you've given me.
Thank you for coming to the rescue.
Thank you for going out of your way to help me.
Thank you for lending me a hand.
Thank you for saving my day.
도와주셔서 **고맙습니다**.

2 **Congratulations on** _____. ~을 축하합니다.

① your success on the project
② becoming the bureau chief
③ the birth of your son

▶ 프로젝트의 성공을 / 지국장이 되신 것을 / 당신 아들의 출산을

3 **I appreciate** _____. ~에 감사드립니다.

① all the help you've given me
② your quick response
③ your efficiency

▶ 제게 주신 많은 도움에 / 빠른 응답에 / 효율적인 업무처리에

24.mp3

A ¹**I heard about** the stock market crash. Did it affect your business a lot?

B Yeah, it caused a lot of problems.

A ²**I can commiserate** with you **on** that. My business has been bad, too.

B Well, ³**I'm sure** we'll be doing better soon.

A Yeah, I know. I'm just afraid things will get worse.

B It's possible. But let's try to think positively.

Pattern Training

1

I heard about ⌐──────────┐.
~에 대해 들었습니다.

① your car accident
② the crisis with your biggest client
③ the demotion

▶ 교통사고 / 주거래 고객이 재정적 위기에 처한 것 / 좌천

응원의 표현

▸ Don't call it quits.
▸ Don't bail out at the first sign of trouble.
▸ Don't throw in the towel.
▸ Hang in there.
포기하지 말고 계속하세요.

2

I can commiserate with ⌐──────────┐ **on** ⌐──────────┐.
~가 …때문에 힘들어하는 것이 안타깝습니다.

① you, your sickness
② her, her husband's death
③ John, his bankruptcy

▶ 당신, 병 / 그녀, 그녀 남편의 죽음 / 존, 그의 파산

3

I'm sure ⌐──────────┐. ~라고 확신합니다.

① he'll do a great job
② it's over
③ there will be quite a change

▶ 그가 대단한 일을 할 것이라고 / 끝났다고 / 많은 변화가 있을 것이라고

A Find the correct responses to complete the dialogs.

1 I'm certain you will see the light at the end of the tunnel.
2 I brought something for you.
3 Thank you for your gift.
4 We just heard about the good news, so we decided to come to congratulate you on your promotion.

Answers
ⓐ Oh, you didn't have to. Thank you very much.
ⓑ Don't mention it.
ⓒ Thank you. It means a lot.
ⓓ I really appreciate it.

B Complete the short dialogs.

1

A: How's your business these days?
B: _____ for me.(모든 게 상당히 어렵습니다.)
   My business hasn't made a profit in a couple of months.
A: That's too bad. _____.(당신 기분을 이해합니다.)
   But don't worry. The economy is starting to improve, so I'm sure that things
   _____.(상황이 곧 호전되어서 나아질 거라 믿어요.)
B: I hope so.

2

A: We _____ of your father's death.
   (당신 아버님이 작고하셨다는 비극적인 소식을 듣게 되어 유감입니다.) I am here to _____
   _____ to you and your family.(당신을 비롯해 가족분들께 조의를 표하기 위해
   왔습니다.) Your father was a wonderful man, and I had the privilege of working
   with him before. Please let me know if there's anything I can do.
B: Thank you. _____.(고맙게 생각합니다.)

A   Listen to the dialog and check true or false.   25.mp3

1   The woman won the employee of the year award.   T   F

2   The woman is surprised that she won the award.   T   F

3   The woman compliments her coworkers for helping her.   T   F

B   Listen again and complete the dialogs.   25.mp3

> Ronald: Nancy, __1_____ ____ _____ _____. You must be so happy to __2_____
> _____ _____ of the year.
>
> Nancy: Thanks so much. I really can't believe that __3____ _____ _____ _____.
>
> Ronald: Why do you say that? You did a great job.
>
> Nancy: Well, I couldn't have done it without the rest of my team. The award __4_____ ____
> ____ _____, not just one person.
>
> Ronald: It's __5_____ _____ ____ _____ to say that.

C   Listen to the dialog and answer the questions.   26.mp3

1   What is wrong with the woman?
> ▶

2   What is the woman going to do?
> ▶

3   What does the man say about the woman's problem?
> ▶

사무기기 다루기

Dealing with Office Equipment

Vocabulary & Expressions

사무기기 이용하기 Using Office Equipment

- **photocopy** 복사하다 (= xerox)
- **photocopier** 복사기 (= copy machine)
- **fax** 팩스를 보내다 (fax machine 팩스 기기)
- **scan** 스캔하다 (scanner 스캐너)
- **be out of order** 고장 나다 (= not be working, break down)
- **make a copy of** ~의 복사본을 만들다
- **get[have] ... fixed** (기계 등을) 고치다
- **tidy up** ~을 정돈하다

🖊 사무용품 office supplies

- paper clips 종이 클립
- ruler 자
- scissors 가위
- paper weight 문진
- desk dairy 탁상용 다이어리
- file 자료철
- stapler 스테이플러
- sticky notes 포스트잇
- recycling paper 이면지 (= used paper)

컴퓨터 이용하기 Using Computers

- **turn the computer on** 컴퓨터의 전원을 켜다 (= start the computer, boot up the computer)
- **be infected with a virus** 바이러스에 감염되다 (= have a virus)
- **remove a virus** 바이러스를 제거하다 (= clean the hard drive)
- **install** 프로그램 등을 깔다 (= load)
- **partition the hard drive** 하드 드라이브를 분할하다
- **insert a flash drive into** ~에 USB 메모리를 꽂다
- **print** (문서를) 출력하다
- **be out of toner** 토너가 다 떨어지다
- **be jammed** (종이 등이) 걸리다, 끼다
- **be down** 다운되다, 연결이 안 되다
- **access the Internet** 인터넷에 접속하다
- **attached file** 첨부 파일

Useful Expressions

Some paper got jammed in the photocopier.	복사기에 종이가 끼었어요.
Could you fax the report?	그 보고서를 팩스로 보내주시겠어요?
We should get someone to fix the scanner.	스캐너를 고칠 사람을 불러야겠습니다.
My computer won't boot up.	컴퓨터 시동이 걸리지 않아요.
My computer is infected with a virus.	컴퓨터가 바이러스에 감염됐어요.

Vocabulary Check-Up

A Match the meanings on the left with the expressions on the right.

1 복사기 · · ⓐ attached file

2 고장 나다 · · ⓑ photocopier

3 프로그램을 깔다 · · ⓒ print

4 출력하다 · · ⓓ not be working

5 첨부 파일 · · ⓔ install

B Fill in the blanks with the given words.

1 복사기에 종이가 걸렸다.

  ▶ Some paper _____ _____ in the photocopier.

2 컴퓨터가 바이러스에 감염됐어요.

  ▶ My computer _____ _____ _____ a virus.

3 제 컴퓨터에는 그 프로그램이 깔려 있지 않아요.

  ▶ The program is _____ _____ on my computer.

4 프린터에 토너가 다 떨어져서 새 카트리지로 교체해야 해요.

  ▶ The printer is _____ _____ _____, so we should replace it with a new cartridge.

> **Words**
> get jammed
> be out of
> be infected with
> install
> toner

C Refer to the Korean and fill in the blanks.

1 Can you _____ these for me? I need two copies each. 저 대신 이것 좀 복사해 주시겠어요? 각각 두 장씩 필요합니다.

2 My computer won't _____. 컴퓨터 작동이 안 돼요.

3 I can't get online. The server must _____ _____. 온라인에 접속이 안 돼요. 서버가 다운된 게 틀림없습니다.

4 You might have to _____ the hard drive and use the recovery disk to _____ it.

  하드 드라이버를 분할해야겠어요. 그래야 재부팅에 필요한 복구 디스크를 사용할 수 있습니다.

5 Please, _____ _____ your desk, and throw some stuff out if you don't need it.

  필요 없는 물건들은 버리고 책상 좀 정리해주세요.

Our company's server has been down all day long.	우리 회사의 (인터넷 / 네트워크) 서버가 하루 종일 **다운입니다**.
I can't access the Internet.	인터넷에 **접속이 안 돼요**.
Print the document, and then make ten copies of it.	문서를 **출력해서** 10장 **복사해 주세요**.
Excel is not installed on my computer.	제 컴퓨터에는 엑셀이 **깔려 있지 않아요**.
There is an attached file in the e-mail.	그 이메일에는 파일이 **첨부되어** 있어요.

27.mp3

A My computer won't start. ¹**I've been trying to** boot it up, **but** it just doesn't work. I'm afraid my computer is infected with a virus.

B Have you checked for viruses lately?

A No, I haven't done that.

B ²**You better** run a virus program as soon as you reboot it, by using the recovery flash drive. Okay?

A Okay, I'll try. By the way, I have to print a document and make some copies of it for the presentation today. But I found that the printer was out of toner. Has the toner been replaced yet?

B I'm not sure about that. If it still is out of toner, you should get a new cartridge from the General Affairs Department.

Pattern Training

1 **I've been trying to** _____ **but** _____. 계속해서 ~해봤지만, ….

① call you all morning, you didn't answer my calls
② get to Asan, I have no idea how to get there
③ make some copies of these documents, the photocopier is not working

▶ 아침 내내 전화했는데, 받질 않더군요 / 아산에 가려고 했는데, 가는 방법을 모르겠어요 / 이 서류들을 몇 부 복사하려 했지만, 복사기가 작동하지 않네요

2 **You better** _____. ~하는 게 좋겠습니다.

① get going now before you miss your plane
② have something to eat before you starve
③ take it easy before you get sick

▶ 비행기를 놓치기 전에 지금 출발하는 게 / 배고프기 전에 뭐 좀 먹는 게 / 병나기 전에 좀 쉬는 게

🔊 도움을 요청하는 표현
- Can you do me a favor?
- Could I ask you a favor?
- Would you mind doing me a favor?
도와주시겠어요?

28.mp3

A　What's wrong?

B　The server's down, and now this paper got jammed in the photocopier. But I don't know how to get it out.

A　**¹Sounds like** you are having a bad day. Let me see…. First you have to open this cover and then slide this part out. After that, just open the cover of the sliding part. Ah, I can see it. Then get the jammed paper out.

B　**²I appreciate** your help. **³I was wondering** who to contact to get someone to fix this.

A　You're welcome. I'm kind of good with machines. Tell me if you need any help.

Pattern Training

1　**Sounds like** ▯▯▯▯▯▯▯. ~인 것 같군요.

① you are sick and tired of it

② you are enjoying the work

③ you are interested in the project

▶ 그것에 신물이 난 것 / 그 일을 즐기고 있는 것 / 그 프로젝트에 관심이 있는 것

2　**I appreciate** ▯▯▯▯▯▯▯. ~에 감사드립니다.

① your kindness

② your hospitality

③ your understanding

▶ 당신의 친절 / 당신의 환대 / 당신의 이해

🔵 진행 순서 표현

▸ First…, second…, third…
첫째…, 둘째…, 셋째…

▸ Firstly…, secondly…, thirdly…
첫째로…, 둘째로…, 셋째로…

▸ First…, then…, next…, after that…, finally/lastly…
처음은…, 그래서…, 다음은…, 그 후에…, 결국…

3　**I was wondering** ▯▯▯▯▯▯▯. ~가 궁금했어요.

① how to use this scanner

② if he could help me with this

③ when we should submit this report

▶ 이 스캐너의 사용법이 / 그가 이것을 도와줄 수 있는지 / 언제 이 보고서를 제출해야 하는지

A Find the correct responses to complete the dialogs.

1 The received faxes are blank.
2 The paper keeps jamming.
3 I think my computer has a virus.
4 Is there any problem with your computer?

Answers
ⓐ I don't know what the problem is. My computer won't start.
ⓑ You'd better scan your computer by using an anti-virus program.
ⓒ I guess this fax is out of toner.
ⓓ Remove the excess paper from the printer tray.

B Complete the short dialogs.

1

A: _____.(인터넷 접속이 하루 종일
안 좋아요.) The computer keeps getting disconnected from the system.

B: Have you tried to call the computer technician? Maybe he can help.

A: Actually, this is a problem throughout our department. The technicians
aren't _____.(기술자도 무엇이 문제인지 정확히 확신하지 못
하더라고요.)

B: That's strange. There are no problems _____
_____.(우리 부서는 인터넷 접속에 문제가 없는데요.)

2

A: I've got to prepare a presentation, but I need to _____
_____.(먼저 이 소프트웨어를 제 컴퓨터에 설치해야 해요.)

B: Don't you know how to install the software yourself?

A: Not really.

B: Okay, first you need to _____.(먼저 컴퓨터에
그 디스크를 넣어야 해요.) Then, it's going to ask you if you want to install the
program. Click "okay" when you get asked that question. It should
_____.(자동으로 설치를 시작할 거예요.)

A: Wow, that's pretty easy. Thanks a lot for your help.

Practice 2 — Listen-up!

A   Listen to the dialog and check true or false.   29.mp3

	True	False
1 The man cannot use the fax machine well.		
2 The first step in sending a fax is to dial the number.		
3 The paper should automatically go through the fax machine.		

B   Listen again and complete the blanks.   29.mp3

Laura: Do you think you can give me a hand here? I don't know __¹_____ _____ _____ _____

       _____ _____.

Daniel: Okay, it's really simple. First, __²_____ _____ _____ _____ _____ _____

       _____ into the tray here.

Laura: That's easy. Then what should I do?

Daniel: Next, __³_____ _____ _____ _____ _____ _____ ____ _____. The fax

       should dial the number automatically.

Laura: Okay, I can hear a ringing sound right now. Oh, what's that horrible noise?

Daniel: That's the sound of the fax machine connecting. Now, your paper __⁴_____ _____

       _____ _____ the machine, and your fax will be sent.

C   Listen to the dialog and answer the questions.   30.mp3

1   What does the man want to borrow from the woman?

▶ _____

2   Why does the man need to borrow that?

▶ _____

3   What does the woman give the man?

▶ _____

Steve Jobs
"The World's Greatest Innovator"

Born in 1955 in San Francisco, Steve Jobs [1]**became an iconic figure** in the world of computing and entertainment. Jobs who once said "Innovation distinguishes between a leader and a follower" became the cofounder and eventual CEO of Apple, and pioneered a set of products that revolutionized how people create, distribute, and consume media around the world.

As a child Jobs [2]**showed a passion for** tinkering. When the family moved to Los Altos, California in 1967 Jobs built on this passion as the area was heavily populated with engineers and their families.

Jobs and high-school friend Steve Wozniak partnered to co-found Apple Computer in 1976, producing the world's first mass-produced graphical-user interface computer (the Macintosh). This [3]**was followed by** the development of the first laser printer (the LaserWriter) in 1985. After a power struggle at Apple, Jobs [4]**was removed from** the board of directors and he left the company. Returning in 1997, he and his design team [5]**were** largely **responsible for** the development of the iMac, iTunes, iTunes Store, Apple Store, iPod, iPhone, and iPad.

In 2003, Jobs [6]**was diagnosed with** pancreatic cancer. But even while in the hospital Jobs was determined to keep working. He continued to sketch ideas for new devices and designs, receiving 141 patents even after he passed away in 2011.

rnkadsgn©Shutterstock

스티브 잡스 ─ "세계 최고의 혁신가"

1955년 샌프란시스코에서 태어난 스티브 잡스는 컴퓨팅과 엔터테인먼트 분야에서 상징적인 인물이 되었다. '혁신은 리더와 추종자를 구분하는 잣대다'라고 말한 잡스는 애플의 공동 설립자이자 CEO가 되었으며, 사람들이 전 세계에서 미디어를 제작, 배포 및 소비하는 방법에 혁명을 일으킨 일련의 제품을 선구적으로 만들었다.

잡스는 어린 시절에 팅커링*에 대한 열정을 보였다. 가족 모두가 1967년 캘리포니아 로스알토스로 이사했을 때, 잡스는 엔지니어가 많은 지역적 특성과 가족의 영향으로 이 열정을 키워 나갔다.

잡스와 고등학교 친구인 스티브 워즈니악은 1976년에 애플컴퓨터를 공동 설립하기 위해 함께했고, 세계 최초 양산화된 그래픽 사용자 인터페이스 컴퓨터인 매킨토시를 생산했다. 그후 1985년에는 최초의 레이저 프린터인 레이저라이터를 개발했다. 애플 내부의 권력 투쟁 후, 잡스는 이사회에서 쫓겨나 회사를 떠났다. 1997년에 다시 애플로 돌아온 그와 그의 디자인 팀은 아이맥, 아이튠즈, 아이튠즈스토어, 애플스토어, 아이팟, 아이폰, 아이패드의 개발을 맡았다.

2003년 잡스는 췌장암 진단을 받았다. 그러나 병원에 있는 동안에도 계속 일하기로 결심했다. 그는 계속해서 새로운 기기와 디자인 아이디어를 구상해 나갔으며, 2011년 그가 세상을 떠난 후에도 그는 141개의 특허를 받았다.

*원래 의미는 '땜질'이나, 최근에는 물건을 만들고 개선, 보완하는 활동을 뜻함.

1 become an iconic figure 상징적인 인물이 되다

Charles Chaplin has **become an iconic figure** in the world's movie history.
찰리 채플린은 전 세계 영화사에 상징적인 인물이 되었다.

2 show a passion for ~에 열정을 보이다

From an early age Emma Watson showed **a passion for** acting.
이른 나이부터 엠마 왓슨은 연기에 열정을 보였다.

3 be followed by ~ 다음에, ~ 뒤를 따라서

▶ 전치사 by 뒤에 나오는 사건이 시간상 더 늦다는 점에 주의하자.

The big party **was followed by** a concert.
파티가 끝난 다음 콘서트가 진행되었다.

4 be removed from ~에서 제거되다

You **will be removed from** our mailing lists within 24 hours.
귀하는 저희 메일링 리스트에서 24시간 이내에 삭제될 것입니다.

5 be responsible for ~에 책임이 있는, 원인이 있는

▶ responsible의 반대말은 irresponsible이지만 이 단어는 '책임이 없는'이라는 뜻보다는 '무책임한'이라는 뜻으로 쓰인다.

He is the one who **is responsible for** what happened.
일어난 일에 대한 책임은 그분에게 있습니다.

6 be diagnosed with ~로 진단받다

Unfortunately, he **has been diagnosed with** lung cancer.
불행히도 그는 폐암으로 진단받았습니다.

Who is Steve Jobs?

'IT업계의 전설'로 불리는 스티브 잡스는 1955년 생후 1주일만에 폴·클라라 잡스 부부에게 입양되었다. 초등학교 때는 학교를 빼먹는 문제아였지만 전자제품 조립에 관심이 많은 청소년기를 보냈다. 오리건주 포틀랜드의 리드대학교에 입학했지만 철학에 흥미를 느끼지 못해 1학기를 마치고 중퇴했다. 1976년에 스티브 워즈니악과 실리콘 밸리에 애플컴퓨터를 공동 설립하여 1977년에는 개인 컴퓨터의 대중화에 성공했고, 1984년에는 매킨토시를 선보였다. 그러나 IBM에 비해 비싼 가격 때문에 성공을 거두지 못하고 1985년 애플 경영 일선에서 물러났다. 이후 넥스트사를 설립하여 그래픽 회사인 픽사를 인수했고, 넥스트사와 애플이 합병되면서 애플의 CEO로 복귀했다. 2000년대 초부터 그가 개발하고 내놓은 제품들은 전 세계적인 열풍을 몰고 왔고, '프리젠테이션의 구재'로 이름을 날렸으며 세계를 놀라게 했다. 그러나 췌장암 진단 이후 병마와 싸우는 중에도 일을 계속하다가 결국 팀 쿡에게 CEO 자리를 물려주고 2011년 네 자녀와 부인을 남겨두고 세상을 떠났다.

Steve Jobs Says...

"Innovation distinguishes between a leader and a follower."
혁신은 리더와 추종자를 구분하는 잣대입니다.

"Sometimes life hits you in the head with a brick. Don't lose faith."
때로는 인생이 여러분의 머리를 벽돌로 치더라도 믿음을 잃지 마십시오.

Taner Muhlis Karaguzel©Shutterstock

General Business
Welcoming Visitors

PART 3
방문객 맞이하기

공항에서 손님 맞이하기

Greeting Visitors at the Airport

Vocabulary & Expressions

손님 맞이하기 Welcoming Visitors

- **get used to** ~에 익숙해지다 (= get accustomed to)
- **pick someone up** ~을 태우러 나가다, 마중 나가다
- **be delayed** (비행기가) 연착되다
- **know someone by one's face** ~와 안면이 있다
- **travel light** 최소한의 짐만 가지고 가볍게 여행하다
- **jet lag** 시차로 인한 피로
- **time difference** 시차
- **stopover** 비행 도중 단기 체류 (= layover)
- **night flight** 야간 비행 (red-eye)
- **baggage** 짐, 수하물
- **suitcase** 여행 가방

> Hello, **you must be** Mr. Jones. **My name is** Mark Clark.
> 안녕하세요, 존스 씨죠? 제 이름은 마크 클라크입니다.

> Oh, **nice to meet you**, Mr. Clark.
> 오, 반가워요, 클라크 씨.

> **Let me help you with your bags.**
> 가방 드는 거 도와 드릴게요.

> Thank you, but **I can manage**.
> 고맙습니다만, 저 혼자도 괜찮아요.

공항에서 호텔까지 From Airport to Hotel

- **reserve a room** 방을 예약하다 (reserve = book)
- **head to** ~로 향하다
- **have a rest** 휴식하다
- **tight schedule** 빡빡한 일정
- **sightseeing** 관광

- **make a reservation for** ~을 예약하다
- **be all set for** ~을 위한 준비가 완료되다
- **show someone around** ~에게 구경시켜 주다
- **business trip** 출장
- **go sightseeing** 관광하다 (= see the sights)

Useful Expressions

It's so nice to finally meet you .	드디어 뵙게 되다니 정말 반갑습니다.
How was your flight?	비행기 여행은 어떠셨어요?
We had a three-hour layover in JFK.	우리는 JFK 공항에 3시간 동안 머물렀습니다.
Is this your first visit to Korea?	한국에는 처음 오신 건가요?
Do you know him by his face ?	그분과 안면이 있으신가요?

Vocabulary Check-Up

A Match the meanings on the left with the expressions on the right.

1 시차로 인한 피로 ·   · ⓐ take a rest

2 비행 도중 단기 체류 ·   · ⓑ suitcase

3 관광하다 ·   · ⓒ go sightseeing

4 여행 가방 ·   · ⓓ jet lag

5 쉬다 ·   · ⓔ stopover

B Fill in the blanks with the given words.

1 제가 하얏트에 이미 객실을 예약했습니다. 괜찮으세요?
   ▶ I already _____ _____ _____ at the Hyatt for you. Is that okay?

2 바이어들을 마중 나가러 공항에 가봐야 합니다.
   ▶ I have to go to the airport to _____ our buyers _____.

3 가방 드는 거 도와 드릴게요.
   ▶ Let me _____ you _____ _____ with your bags.

4 호텔은 예약하셨어요?
   ▶ Did you _____ _____ _____ for the hotel?

> **Words**
> give someone a hand
> pick up
> make a reservation
> book a room

C Refer to the Korean and fill in the blanks.

1 We had a four-hour _____ in Beijing. 우리는 베이징에서 4시간 경유했습니다.

2 Is this your _____ _____ to Korea? 한국에는 처음 방문하시는 겁니까?

3 Shall we get going? I'll _____ you _____ _____ to the hotel. 가실까요? 제가 호텔까지 태워 드리겠습니다.

4 Excuse me, but _____ _____ Mr. White? 실례합니다만, 화이트 씨 아니세요?

5 The flight _____ _____ a little. 비행기가 약간 연착했습니다.

I'll give you a ride to the hotel.   호텔까지 태워 드리겠습니다.

Let me carry one of your bags for you .   가방 하나는 제가 들어 드릴게요.

I booked a room at the Century Plaza Hotel just in case.   만약을 대비해 센츄리 플라자 호텔에 방을 예약해 놓았습니다.

So, are you all set for the conference?   그럼, 컨퍼런스 준비는 다 되었습니까?

It shouldn't take any longer than half an hour.   30분 이상은 안 걸릴 겁니다.

31.mp3

A Mr. Richardson? My name is Carol, Carol Green. We've spoken on the phone before.

B Yes, Ms. Green. How are you?

A Good. ¹**It's so nice to finally** meet you. So, how was your journey to Korea?

B It wasn't too bad. It was a very long flight though.

A Yes, ²**it will take a while before** you get used to the time difference. Well, ³**I'll give** you **a ride to** the hotel. Let me take one of your bags.

B Thank you. Is the hotel close to the conference hall?

A Yes, it is. So it should be convenient enough for you.

B That sounds great.

Pattern Training

1 **It's so nice to finally** [_____]. 마침내 ~해서 좋군요.

① go on a vacation
② change jobs
③ get a bonus

▶ 휴가를 가서 / 이직해서 / 보너스를 받아서

2 **It will take a while before** [_____]. ~하기까지 시간이 좀 걸릴 겁니다.

① he can get to work
② the overall results of this study are analyzed
③ everything is set up completely

▶ 그가 출근할 수 있기까지 / 이 연구의 전체적인 결과가 분석되기까지 / 모든 것이 완벽하게 준비되기까지

3 **I'll give** [_____] **a ride to** [_____]. …을 ~까지 태워다 드릴게요.

① the client, the station
② my friends, the post office
③ the managing director, the convention center

▶ 고객을, 역까지 / 친구들을, 우체국까지 / 전무이사를, 컨벤션 센터까지

32.mp3

A [1]**Is this your first visit to** Korea?

B Yes, I'm kind of excited. By the way, is the hotel far from here?

A No, [2]**it shouldn't take more than** half an hour from here. I booked a room at the Blueridge Hotel because it's convenient. I hope you don't mind the Blueridge Hotel.

B That will be just fine. Thank you.

A Anyway, you will have some time to yourself at the hotel before everything begins.

B Fantastic. I'll take a shower and then head out to your company.

Pattern Training

1   **Is this your first visit to** [　　　　　　]**?** ~에는 처음 오신 건가요?

① Saudi Arabia
② Italy
③ Busan

▶ 사우디아라비아 / 이탈리아 / 부산

2   **It shouldn't take more than** [　　　　　　]**.** ~(시간) 이상 걸리진 않을 겁니다.

① a few days
② an hour
③ about 45 minutes to get there

▶ 며칠 / 한 시간 / 거기 도착하는 데 약 45분

🔊 호텔 위치를 묻는 표현

- Is the hotel far(close) from here?
  호텔이 여기서 멉니까?(가깝습니까?)
- Is the hotel near here?
  호텔이 여기서 가까운가요?
- Does it take long to get to the hotel from here?
  여기서 호텔까지 오래 걸리나요?

Practice 1 — Let's Speak!

A Find the correct responses to complete the dialogs.

1 I'm going to the airport to pick the buyer up.
2 It must be because of jet lag. I feel quite tired.
3 How was your journey to Korea?
4 We had a three-hour layover in JFK.
5 Let me take one of your bags.
6 Excuse me, aren't you Mr. and Ms. Watson of the iWorld Company?

Answers
ⓐ Yes, we are.
ⓑ It was pretty uneventful.
ⓒ Okay. Do you know him by his face?
ⓓ That's very thoughtful of you.
ⓔ Three hours isn't too bad.
ⓕ Yes, it will take a while before you get used to the time difference.

B Complete the short dialogs.

1

A: _____.(Hyatt Hotel에 방을 예약해 두었습니다.)
Many people who have stayed there have told me the rooms are really nice there. I hope _____.
(Hyatt Hotel이 마음에 드셨으면 좋겠네요.)

B: That will be just fine. Thank you.

A: Anyway, you will have some time to yourself before the meeting begins.

B: Fantastic. I'd like to _____.
(그럼 좀 더 편한 옷으로 갈아입고 싶네요.)

2

A: It won't _____.(호텔에 도착하는 데 오래
걸리지 않을 겁니다.) That means you will have some time to yourself before
everything starts. So _____
(샤워하시거나 쉴 수 있어요) before we _____
(저희 회사로 출발하기 전에) if you like once we get to the hotel.

B: That's _____.(사려 깊으시군요) Thank you.

A   Listen to the dialog and answer the questions.   33.mp3

	True	False
1 This conversation takes place in a car.		
2 The client's last name is Mr. Davis.		
3 The speakers have met before.		
4 The hotel is closer to the company than the convention center.		

B   Listen again and complete the blanks.   33.mp3

Nancy: Mr. Davis? __¹___ _____ ____ Nancy, Nancy Brown. We've spoken on the phone before.

Mr. Davis: Ah, Ms. Brown. __²_____ _____ _____ to finally meet you.

Nancy: The pleasure __³_____ _____ _____. Please call me Nancy. So did you __⁴_____ _____ _____?

Mr. Davis: Yes, but I'm still __⁵___ _____ _____.

Nancy: Right. I hope you will feel better soon. This way, Mr. Davis. There's a car __⁶_____ _____ _____ outside.

Mr. Davis: Is the Hilton Hotel __⁷___ _____ _____ _____?

Nancy: It __⁸_____ _____ _____ _____ _____ by car, but the convention center is a little far from the hotel. But don't worry. __⁹____ _____ _____ _____ _____ whenever you need to go during your stay.

Mr. Davis: That's very kind of you. Thank you.

비즈니스 미팅 준비하기

Preparing for Business Meetings

Vocabulary & Expressions

일정 확인하기 Checking the Itinerary

- **itinerary** 여행 스케줄
- **personal organizer** 개인용 전자수첩
- **timeframe** 일정, (행동·계획에 관한) 시간의 틀
- **in advance** 미리, 사전에
- **prior to** ~에 앞서, 먼저 (prioritize 우선순위를 매기다)
- **ahead of schedule** 예정보다 빠른 (↔ behind schedule 예정보다 지체된)
- **on schedule** 예정대로
- **delay** 지체하다, 지연
- **make up the (lost) time** 누수된 시간을 만회하다
- **be scheduled to** ~할 예정이다
- **be supposed to** ~하기로 되어 있다
- **brief A on B** B에 대해 A에게 간략히 말하다
- **be subject to** ~하기 쉽다
- **feel free to ask** 자유롭게 질문하다

🔊 부서

- Marketing Department 마케팅부
- Human Resources Department 인사부
- R&D Department 연구개발부
- Accounting Department 경리부

🔊 직위

- Chairman 회장
- President 사장
- CEO 최고경영자
- Vice President 부사장
- Managing Director 전무이사
- Supervisor 감독(관리)
- Manager 부장
- Section Chief 과장
- Assistant Manager 주임(대리)
- Staff 직원
- Clerk 점원

다른 사람 소개하기 Introducing Others

- **I'd like to introduce A.** A를 소개합니다. (= I'd like you to meet A.)
- **You can call me A.** A라고 불러주세요.
- **colleague** 동료 (= co-worker)
- **business card** 명함
- **boss** 상사
- **customer** 손님
- **be out of** ~이 바닥나다 (= run out of)
- **senior** 선임자
- **client** 고객

Useful Expressions

What's the timeframe for this trip?

We are ahead of schedule , so we can take a short break.

Can you let me know in advance?

The schedule is now subject to change due to the bad weather.

I'd like to introduce Steve Park of Novelle International to you.

이 견학에 대한 **일정**은 어떻습니까?

일정보다 빠르니 잠시 쉬어도 되겠습니다.

미리 알려 주시겠습니까?

현재 악천후로 인해 **일정이 변동될 수 있습니다.**

노벨레 인터네셔널 사의 스티브 박 씨를 **소개합니다.**

Vocabulary Check-Up

A Match the meanings on the left with the expressions on the right.

1 개인용 전자수첩 ·   · ⓐ Accounting Department

2 선임자, 선배 ·   · ⓑ business card

3 동료 ·   · ⓒ personal organizer

4 경리부 ·   · ⓓ colleague

5 명함 ·   · ⓔ senior

B Fill in the blanks with the given words.

1 전시회 일정은 어떻게 됩니까?
▶ What's the ＿＿＿＿＿＿ for the exhibition?

2 걱정하지 마십시오. 저희는 예정대로 진행 중입니다.
▶ Don't worry. We are right ＿＿＿ ＿＿＿＿＿.

3 예정보다 늦었으니 빨리 출발하는 게 좋겠군요.
▶ We are ＿＿＿＿＿ ＿＿＿＿＿＿, so we'd better get going very soon.

4 제 명함이 다 떨어졌어요. 다음에 드려도 괜찮을까요?
▶ I'm all ＿＿＿ ＿＿ my business cards. Will it be okay if I give one to you another time?

> **Words**
> behind schedule
> timeframe
> on schedule
> out of

C Refer to the Korean and fill in the blanks.

1 We ＿＿＿ ＿＿＿＿＿ ＿＿＿ tour the manufacturing facility today. 오늘은 제조 시설을 순회하기로 예정되어 있습니다.

2 ＿＿＿＿ has been a ＿＿＿＿ in our schedule. 저희 일정에 변동이 생겼습니다.

3 In reply to your inquiry, I am sending you the ＿＿＿＿＿. 귀하의 질문에 대한 회답으로, 방문 일정표를 보내드립니다.

4 ＿＿＿＿ ＿＿ my colleague Mr. Fisher. 이분은 제 동료인 피셔 씨입니다.

5 Please ＿＿＿＿ ＿＿＿＿ to ask me questions any time. 언제라도 자유롭게 질문해 주세요.

This is my colleague Michael.	제 동료인 마이클**입니다**.
Please call me Michael.	마이클이라고 **불러주세요**.
Here's my (business) card.	여기 제 **명함입니다**.
I'm all out of business cards.	명함이 모두 **떨어졌네요**.
He is senior to me in the company .	그는 제 **선임입니다**.

34.mp3

A **¹What's the timeframe for** the exhibition?

B **²My manager is trying to** construct the timescale of events leading up to the exhibition. When we get the final schedule, we will let you know in advance.

A Thank you. It sounds like you've been having a very tough time with the tight schedule and all that.

B You can say that again. Let me check the itinerary and see what time the factory tour is scheduled. Oh, **³we are ahead of schedule, so we** can take a short break if you like. I believe we are one hour ahead of schedule.

A A break sounds great. I could do with a coffee.

Pattern Training \

1　**What's the timeframe for** [＿＿＿＿＿＿＿＿]**?** ~의 일정은 어떻게 됩니까?

① the seminar
② the conference
③ the training

▶ 세미나 / 컨퍼런스 / 훈련

2　**My manager is trying to** [＿＿＿＿＿＿＿].
저희 부장님께서 ~하기 위해 노력 중입니다.

① reschedule the meeting
② organize a dinner party for the new clients
③ get a contract with PNG

▶ 회의 시간을 다시 정하기 위해 / 새로운 고객들을 위한 저녁 파티를 준비하기 위해 / PNG사와 계약을 맺기 위해

🔵 적극적으로 동의할 때

- You can say that again.
- You said it.
- Tell me about it.
- You're telling me.
- You read my mind.
  두말하면 잔소리지요.

3　**We are ahead of schedule, so we** [＿＿＿＿＿＿＿]. 일정보다 앞서 있으니, ~.

① can take it easy
② don't have to rush like that
② don't have to worry about being late

▶ 여유를 가져도 되겠습니다 / 그렇게 서둘 필요 없습니다 / 늦을까 봐 걱정하지 않아도 됩니다

35.mp3

A Hi, Fiona. How's it going?

B Very well. Thank you. Spencer, **this is** my colleague Kaden. We started working here at the same time, but he's senior to me in the company. **He used to work** at the Jeju branch **before** he came to Seoul.

A Hello, Kaden, You can call me Spencer.

C Hello, Spencer. It's nice to meet you.

A It's good to meet you too. I'm all out of business cards.
   Would it be okay if I give one to you the next time we meet?

C Sure. Here's my business card.

A Thank you.

Pattern Training

1 **This is** [_____]. 이분은 ~입니다.

① one of our clients, Mr. Smith
② our associate from Vietnam, Ms. Dong
③ my director Ms. Park

▶ 저희 고객 중 한 분인 스미스 씨 / 저희 베트남 친구인 동 씨 / 저희 박 이사님

2 **He used to work** [_____] **before** [_____].
그는 ~전에 …에서 일했었습니다.

① at the Berlin post, he came to Seoul
② at the local branch of a large bank, he came to our company
③ in one of our affiliate companies, he joined us

▶ 서울로 오기 전에, 베를린 지국에서 / 저희 회사로 오기 전에, 큰 은행의 지점에서 / 우리 팀에 합류하기 전에, 계열사 중 한 곳에서

3 **Would it be okay if I** [_____]? 제가 ~해도 괜찮을까요?

① postpone the meeting
② leave earlier
③ give you my honest opinion on that

▶ 회의를 연기해도 / 일찍 떠나도 / 그것에 관해 솔직한 저의 의견을 말해도

A Find the correct responses to complete the dialogs.

1　What's the timeframe for the exhibition?

2　We are ahead of schedule, so we can take a short break if you like.

3　Mr. Smith, this is Mr. Kim, the manager of the Research and Development Division.

4　Here's my business card. Please e-mail me if you can so we can stay in touch.

Answers

ⓐ They are still working on making one right now.

ⓑ I'm glad to meet you. I've heard a lot about you from Ms. Jones.

ⓒ A break sounds great. I could do with a coffee.

ⓓ Absolutely. Here is mine.

B Complete the short dialogs.

1

A: I think we should _____.

(출발하기 전에 오늘의 스케줄을 얘기해야겠습니다.)

B: Okay. What are we planning to do?

A: _____. (10시에 차로 여기를 출발할 겁니다.)

and should reach the Incheon plant by 10:30. After looking around the plant, we're _____.

(저녁 5시까지 다시 여기로 돌아오는 것으로 예정되어 있습니다.)

B: That sounds good enough to me. Let's get started.

2

A: I know we are supposed to visit our plant in Incheon. But I think _____

_____.(다음 주로 방문을 미뤄야겠습니다.)

B: Why _____?(일정이 왜 바뀐 거죠?)

A: Unfortunately, the electricity at the plant has gone out _____

_____.(큰 태풍 때문에 전력 공급이 끊겼습니다.)

B: I'm so sorry to hear that. Anyway, I hope we can look around the plant soon.

A Listen to the dialog and answer the questions. 36.mp3

1 What's the purpose of Ms. Maura's visit?

▶

2 What is the client's English name?

▶

3 Where is the client from?

▶

B Listen again and complete the blanks. 36.mp3

Mark: I don't think _1_____ _____ Ms. Maura. She is one of our clients, and she's from Spain. She has come to our head office to see how we maintain our production line.

Dongsu: Hello, Ms. Maura. I'm Dongsu Jeong. Please _2_____ _____ _____.

Ms. Maura: Hello, Dongsu. My name is Patricia Maura, but _3_____ _____ _____ _____ _____ _____. So you can call me Pat.

Dongsu: Oh, that sounds easier for me. So, _4_____ _____ _____ _____? Did you come from Barcelona?

Ms. Maura: No, from Madrid. _5_____ _____ _____ _____?

Dongsu: No, but I'd love to go there one day.

Ms. Maura: Good. It's a nice place. I think you will like it there.

Dongsu: Great. Here's _6_____ _____ _____.

회사 소개와 공장 견학

Introduction of the Company and Tour of the Plant

Vocabulary & Expressions

회사 소개 Introduction of the Company

- **company history** 회사 연혁
- **be founded in ... by ~** ~에 의해 …년도에 창립되다
- **head office** 본사 **branch** 지점
- **be located in** ~에 위치하다 (= be based in)
- **main product** 주력 상품 (= core product)
- **annual sales** 연간 매출 (net profit 순이익, gross profit 총 수익)
- **subsidiary** 자회사
- **affiliate** 제휴를 맺다
- **workforce** (기업 등의) 노동력
- **company organization** 회사 조직
- **turnover** 일정 기간의 거래량(액), 총매상고
- **specialize in** ~을 전문적으로 다루다
- **per annum** 한 해에 (= a year)
- **workshop** 작업장, 일터
- **on the outskirts of** ~의 변두리에

회사의 주력 분야

- distribution 유통업
- manufacturing 제조업
- construction 건축업
- telecommunication 통신업
- financial business 금융업
- auto industry 자동차 산업
- retail trades 소매업
- semiconductor 반도체

공장 견학 Tour of the Plant

- **employee** 직원
- **plant** 공장 (= factory)
- **manufacturing facility** 제조 시설, 생산 설비
- **manufacture** 제조하다
- **quality control** 품질관리

- **full-time worker** 정규 직원 **part-time worker** 시간제 근무 직원
- **work in three shifts** 3교대로 일하다
- **look around** 둘러보다
- **talk through the tour** 시찰(견학) 내내 설명하다
- **produce** 생산하다, 제조하다 (= turn out)

Useful Expressions

Our company was founded in 1978.
저희 회사는 1978년에 설립되었습니다.

Our head office is located in Washington.
저희 본사는 워싱턴에 있습니다.

The main product of our company is electric home appliances.
저희 회사의 주력 상품은 가전제품입니다.

Our company has a gross profit of over $3 million.
저희 회사는 3백만 달러 이상의 총수익을 올렸습니다.

We have approximately a quarter of a million employees.
저희 회사엔 대략 25만 명의 직원이 있습니다.

A Match the meanings on the left with the expressions on the right.

1	노동 인력 ·	· ⓐ	turnover
2	거래량 ·	· ⓑ	quality control
3	자회사 ·	· ⓒ	workforce
4	품질관리 ·	· ⓓ	subsidiary
5	주력 상품 ·	· ⓔ	core product

B Fill in the blanks with the given words.

1 그 회사는 1971년에 설립됐습니다.

▶ The company _____ _____ ____ 1971.

2 저희 제품은 혁신적인 디자인으로 좋은 평판을 얻고 있습니다.

▶ Our products have a _____ _____ for having innovative designs.

3 저희 생산 설비들을 둘러보러 가시죠.

▶ Let's go and _____ _____ our manufacturing facilities.

4 본사는 광주에 있습니다.

▶ Our head office _____ _____ ____ Gwangju.

Words
be based in
good reputation
look around
be founded in

C Refer to the Korean and fill in the blanks.

1 I'd like to tell you about our _____ _____. 저희 회사의 연혁을 말씀드리겠습니다.

2 This _____ is increasingly running out of workers. 이 작업장에는 점점 근로자들 수가 부족합니다.

3 We have _____ in Hong Kong, Malaysia, and some East Asian countries.
저희는 홍콩과 말레이시아, 그리고 일부 동아시아 국가에 지점이 있습니다.

4 Our company has a _____ _____ of 62 million dollar. 저희 회사는 6천2백만 달러의 총수익을 올렸습니다.

5 Our employees here are working _____ _____ _____. 우리 직원들은 3교대로 일하고 있습니다.

Our company has a good reputation for its innovative marketing strategies.	저희 회사는 혁신적인 마케팅 전략으로 좋은 평판을 얻고 있습니다.
Could you tell us about the NWE Company?	NWE 사에 대해 말씀해 주시겠어요?
What's the main field of your business now?	현재 사업의 주요 분야는 무엇입니까?
What are your profits like?	수익은 어떻습니까?
People here are working in three shifts .	여기 직원들은 3교대로 일하고 있습니다.

37.mp3

A [1]**Could you tell us about** your company?

B Sure. It was founded in 1971, and we have approximately a quarter of a million employees.

A What about your gross profit?

B We have a gross profit of over $150 million per annum.

A I have one more question to ask you. Where is the head office?

B It's based in Inchon, which is on the outskirts of Seoul.

A That's interesting. [2]**I would have thought** the head office would be in Seoul.

B [3]**It is located in** that city for many reasons. One of the reasons is that having the port so close to our office makes managing shipments easier and more efficient.

Pattern Training

1

Could you tell us about [_____]?
~에 대해 말씀해 주시겠습니까?

① the process of the production line
② what you just said in detail
③ the clients we are about to meet

▶ 생산라인의 과정 / 말씀한 내용을 상세히 / 저희가 만나려는 고객들

🔘 회사 설립 연도 말하기
- Our company **was founded** in 1971.
- Our company **got off the ground** in 1971.
- We **started up** in 1971.
- Our company **was established** in 1971.
저희 회사는 1971년에 **설립되었습니다**.

2

I would have thought [_____].
~라고 생각했는데요.

① you would want to look around the office alone
② you would want to eat before we continue with the tour
③ you would dress up more since our CEO is in the meeting

▶ 혼자 사무실을 둘러보시길 원할 거라고 / 견학을 계속하기 전에 식사하시길 원할 거라고 / 회의에 저희 CEO가 참석하므로 좀 더 단정히 차려입으실 거라고

3

It is located in [_____]. ~에 위치해 있습니다.

① an urban area just outside of Seoul
② the center of Busan
③ Jongno

▶ 서울 근처의 도시 / 부산의 중심 / 종로

38.mp3

A You've seen our head office so far, so ¹**let me show you** our workshop now. I'll talk you through the tour, but you can ask me questions any time. ²**Shall we get going to look at** the shop floor?

B After you, sir.

A This is our main operating room. We produce the mainframe here. There are over 200 full-time and 100 part-time workers working here, and, not like some sweatshops, they work in three shifts.

B So you don't overwork them.

A ³**One of many things I'd like to tell you is that** we are very proud of the quality of our products and the sophistication and the high morale of our staff.

B That sounds great. I'd love to work here as well!

Pattern Training

1 **Let me show you** _____. ~을 보여 드리겠습니다.

① how it's done
② the operating system
③ the fundamental structure of all this

▶ 작동 방법 / 운영 체제 / 이것의 전반적인 기본 구조

2 **Shall we get going to look at** _____? ~을 둘러보러 가실까요?

① the showroom
② the boardroom
③ the R&D center

▶ 전시실 / 회의실 / 연구개발 센터

3 **One of many things I'd like to tell you is that** _____.
제가 말씀드리고 싶은 많은 것 중 하나는 ~라는 것입니다.

① this system allows you to cut fuel costs drastically
② this is more durable than other models that are similar
③ it's more convenient than the previous model

▶ 이 시스템은 연료비용을 대폭 절감시켜준다는 것 / 유사한 다른 모델들보다 내구력이 있다는 것 / 이전 모델보다 더 간편하다는 것

A Find the correct responses to complete the dialogs.

1 When was the company founded?
2 Where is the head office?
3 What is the main product of your company?
4 How large is your company in Korea?
5 Why aren't there many workers here?

Answers
ⓐ It was founded in 1971.
ⓑ We produce the core parts of semiconductors.
ⓒ We're the 3rd largest cosmetics manufacturer in Korea.
ⓓ It's based in Incheon, which is on the outskirts of Seoul.
ⓔ Because it's equipped with state-of-the-art industrial robots.

B Complete the short dialogs.

1

A: Could you tell us about your company?
B: Sure. It _____, and we have _____
_____.(1971년에 설립되었고, 약 50만 명의 근로자를 두고 있습니다.)
A: What about your gross profit?
B: We have _____.
(연간 매출 총액이 7천만 달러를 넘습니다.)
A: I have one more question to ask you. Where is the head office?
B: _____.(워싱턴에 있습니다.)

2

A: How big is your company?
B: We're _____,(저희는 두 번째로 큰 스
포츠 신발 제조업체입니다) and we have about four thousand employees.
A: _____?(시장 점유율은 어떤가요?)
B: If I'm not mistaken, _____.
(작년에 35%가 넘었습니다.)

A   Listen to the dialog and check true or false.   39.mp3

	True	False
1 Ms. Simmons will lead Mr. Hills on a tour.		
2 They are going to visit the factory floor first.		
3 The parts manufactured at the factory are for domestic only.		

B   Listen again and complete the blanks.   39.mp3

Mr. Hills: Good morning, Ms. Simmons. I'm glad __¹_____ _____ _____ _____ _____.

Ms. Simmons: It's good to see you, Mr. Hills. So, what are you going to show me this morning?

Mr. Hills: I'm taking you _²_____ _____ _____ _____ _____ _____. This will let you see

firsthand what we do here.

Ms. Simmons: Okay. What are we going to do first?

Mr. Hills: I thought we would visit the factory floor first. You can look _³____ _____ _____

_____ our products.

Ms. Simmons: That sounds good. What products do you make here?

Mr. Hills: _⁴_____ _____ _____, we manufacture lots of small electronic parts.

We ship them to numerous other places overseas

_⁵_____ _____ _____ _____ _____ _____.

+ **BIZ TIPs**   방문 뒤에는 감사 편지를 보내자

거래 회사의 초대를 받아 방문한 뒤에는 간단한 감사의 메시지를 보내는 것이 좋다.

▸ **Thank you very much for** showing us around your company. (귀사를 안내해 주셔서 감사합니다.) [비격식체]

▸ **We appreciate the hospitality** that you showed us when you took us on the tour of your company.
(귀사를 견학했을 때 보여주신 환대에 감사드립니다.)

▸ **On behalf of** all the members who attended the meeting, **I'd like to thank you for giving us the opportunity** to learn about your company. (미팅에 참석한 모든 직원을 대표하여 귀사를 알 수 있는 기회를 주신 것에 대해 감사드리고 싶습니다.) [격식체]

한국 문화 소개하기

Introducing Korean Culture

Vocabulary & Expressions

한국음식과 술 Korean Food & Drinks

- **full course Korean meal** 한정식
- **local specialty** 지역 특산물
- **side dish** 반찬(곁들이는 요리)
- **chopsticks** 젓가락
- **spoon** 숟가락
- **traditional liquor** 전통주
- **grain wine** 곡주
- **with both hands** 두 손으로
- **have a drink** (술) 한잔하다
- **give it a try** 시도해 보다, 먹어보다

가볼 곳 The Place to Go

- **tourist attraction** 관광지
- **historic site** 사적
- **tour guide** 여행 가이드
- **(stone) pagoda** 석탑
- **old palace** 고궁
- **antique** 골동품
- **national museum** 국립박물관
- **folk village** 민속마을
- **national treasure** 국보

추천 한국음식

- **bulgogi** (marinated thin-sliced meat) 불고기
- **galbi** (marinated short ribs) 갈비
- **bibimbap** (cooked rice with assorted vegetables and fried egg on top) 비빔밥
- **kimchi** (pickled cabbage) 김치
- **naengmyun** (cold noodles) 냉면

음식 맛을 나타내는 형용사

- **spicy** 매운
- **greasy** 기름진
- **sweet** 달콤한
- **sour** 신, 시큼한
- **bland** 싱거운
- **salty** 짠
- **fishy** 비린내 나는
- **savory** 향긋한, 풍미 있는

살 것

- **handicrafts** 수공예품
- **bargain** 특가품
- **souvenir** 기념품

Useful Expressions

Do you have any plans for tonight?	오늘 밤 **무슨 계획이라도** 있으신가요?
Shall we go out (together) for dinner?	**(함께) 저녁 먹으러 나가실래요?**
I'd like to try a local specialty.	지역 특산품을 먹어보고 싶습니다.
What is a well-known Korean dish?	**유명한** 한국음식으로 뭐가 있죠?
Are there any vegetarian dishes on the menu?	**메뉴에 채식주의자를 위한** 음식이 있나요?

A Match the meanings on the left with the expressions on the right.

1 한정식 •   • ⓐ side dish

2 반찬 •   • ⓑ full-course Korean meal

3 관광 명소 •   • ⓒ handicrafts

4 전통주 •   • ⓓ traditional liquor

5 수공예품 •   • ⓔ tourist attraction

B Fill in the blanks with the given words.

Words
have a drink
join
have any plans
free
for dinner
well-known

1 안 바쁘시다면 저희와 함께 저녁식사 하시겠어요?

▶ Would you like to _____ us _____ _____ if you are not busy?

2 유명한 한국음식은 뭐가 있어요?

▶ What is a _____ Korean dish?

3 한가하실 때 함께 술 한잔 할 수 있을까요?

▶ Can we _____ ____ _____ together when your're _____?

4 오늘 밤 무슨 계획이라도 있으세요?

▶ Do you _____ _____ _____ for tonight?

C Refer to the Korean and fill in the blanks.

1 Are you interested in _____ ____ _____ _____ of Seoul? 서울 야간관광에 관심 있어요?

2 What's the most famous _____ _____ for Koreans? 한국인들에게 가장 유명한 관광지는 어딘가요?

3 I heard that Korean food is a little _____. 한국음식은 좀 맵다고 들었습니다.

4 Are there any _____ _____ on the menu? 채식주의자를 위한 메뉴가 있나요?

5 Would you like to visit an _____ _____ in Seoul with me? 저와 함께 서울에 있는 고궁에 가보실래요?

How did you like our traditional food?   저희의 전통음식이 **어떻습니까?**

Thank you for inviting me out for dinner.   저녁 외식에 **초대해 주셔서 감사합니다.**

You might want to visit the Korean Folk Village.   한국 민속촌은 **가볼 만합니다.**

Are you interested in taking a night tour of Seoul?   서울 야간관광을 하는 것에 **관심 있으세요?**

Is there any place to you want visit while you're here?   여기 머무는 동안 **가보고 싶은 곳이 있으세요?**

40.mp3

A Hey, Michelle, would you like to join us for dinner if you are not busy?

B That would be lovely. Thank you.

A ¹**Have you ever** tried *bulgogi* before?

B No, I have not. ²**Would you like to** explain what *bulgogi* is?

A It's marinated thin-sliced meat. *Bulgogi* ³**is popular among** foreigners.

B Okay. I should give it a try. Are we going to have a drink?

A Oh, maybe we could have a glass or two of soju. But there's nobody who is a heavy drinker in our party. So don't worry.

B Good. I'm relieved to hear that.

Pattern Training

1 **Have you ever** [＿＿＿＿＿]**?** 전에 ~해보신 적 있어요?

① been to London
② used the Photoshop program
③ worked with Thomas

▶ 런던에 가본 / 포토샵 프로그램을 사용해본 / 토마스와 일해본

2 **Would you like to** [＿＿＿＿＿]**?** ~해 주시겠어요?

① meet me at 2 p.m.
② give me the receipt
③ get going now

▶ 오후 2시에 만나 / 영수증을 주 / 지금 가

3 [＿＿＿＿＿] **is popular among** [＿＿＿＿＿]**.** ~는 …사이에 인기가 있습니다.

① Online dating, single men and women
② Social networking, business people
③ The hotel, travelers

▶ 온라인 만남은 독신 남녀들 사이에 / 사회적 정보망은 사업가들 사이에 / 그 호텔은 여행객들 사이에

41.mp3

A   Do you have any plans after this?

B   Nothing in particular. I will go back to the hotel and get some rest.

A   Then, now that you have tried Korean food, **¹why don't we** go to a Korean tourist attraction near here?

B   Great. Do you know anywhere you'd like to recommend?

A   There is Insadong in Jongno, a very popular place among foreign visitors. You can experience traditional Korean culture in Insadong. This includes Korean paintings, handicrafts, traditional clothing, and ceramics.

B   **²That sounds** interesting. **³Maybe I could** shop for some souvenirs there as well.

A   Good! Let's hurry before it gets dark.

Pattern Training

1   **Why don't we** [_____]**?** ~하는 게 어때요?

① try some spicy food
② finish the report before lunch
③ move to the meeting room to discuss this

▶ 뭔가 매운 음식을 먹어보는 게 / 점심 전에 보고서 작성 먼저 마치는 게 / 회의실로 자리를 옮겨서 이것을 논의하는 게

2   **That sounds** [_____]**.** ~할 것 같군요.

① exciting
② terrible
③ boring

▶ 흥미로울 것 / 매우 안 좋을 것 / 지루할 것

3   **Maybe I could** [_____]**.** 아마도 ~할 수 있을 거예요.

① be a presenter on behalf of him
② cook some Korean food for Mr. Brown
③ leave a message if you are not in

▶ 제가 그를 대신해 발표할 / 브라운 씨를 위해 한국음식을 요리할 / 만약 안 계시면 메시지를 남겨놓을

A Find the correct responses to complete the dialogs.

1 Would you like to join us for dinner if you are not busy?

2 Do you have any plans for tonight?

3 Do you know any attraction and sights you'd like to recommend?

4 Did you enjoy the food? How did you like it?

5 How about going to see the night view of Seoul after work?

Answers

ⓐ Terrific. Let's get the work done quickly then.

ⓑ Well, I really haven't thought about it yet.

ⓒ Thank you. I'd like that very much.

ⓓ Have you ever heard of *Gyungbokgung*? It's a very popular place.

ⓔ I liked it. It was different.

B Complete the short dialog.

A: Are you free this evening?

B: Yes, _____¹_____.(다른 계획 안 만들었어요.)

A: I'd like to _____²_____.(저녁 외식에 모시고 싶은데요.)

B: That sounds great. Thank you.

A: How about *bibimbap*? It is cooked _____³_____.
(쌀밥에 여러 야채가 섞여서 나와요.) It's good for vegetarians.

B: Oh, _____⁴_____.(한번 먹어보고 싶군요.)

+ BIZ TIPs 간단한 인사 표현 알아두기

▶ "감사합니다" 정도는 상대방의 모국어로 알아두자

글로벌 비즈니스는 영어로 진행되는 경우가 많지만 거래하는 국가는 다를 수 있다. 해외 출장을 가기 전에 '안녕하세요', '고맙습 니다' 같은 간단한 표현은 그 나라 말로 알아두면 더 좋은 인상을 줄 수 있다. 또는 상대에게 How do you say 'thank you' in Korean?(한국어로 thank you는 어떻게 말하나요?)와 같이 물어볼 수 있다.

▶ Nice to meet you.와 Nice meeting you.는 하늘과 땅 차이

누군가를 처음 만났을 때와 만난 후 헤어질 때의 인사 표현이 다르다. 처음 만났을 땐 It's nice to meet you.(만나서 반갑습니다.)라고 말하며, 헤어질 때는 It was nice meeting you.(만나서 반가웠습니다.)라고 말한다. to meet과 meeting은 이렇게 큰 차이가 있으니 혼동하지 않도록 주의하자.

A Listen to the dialog and check true or false. 42.mp3

1 The conversation takes place in a Koran traditional restaurant. [T] [F]

2 The visitor is satisfied with the new experience with the food. [T] [F]

3 They will move to another place for sightseeing. [T] [F]

B Listen again and complete the blanks. 42.mp3

The host: So, ¹_____ _____ _____ _____ our Korean traditional food?

Visitor: It was great. I love having variety when it comes to food. ²_____ _____
_____ _____ _____ out to dinner.

The host: I'm glad that you enjoyed everything.

Visitor: Wow, is that the time? I've ³_____ _____ _____ _____.
Thank you again for the lovely dinner. I've really ⁴_____ _____ _____ _____
as well.

The host: I hope we can stay in touch.

C Listen to the dialog and answer the questions. 43.mp3

1 Why does the woman not know about Seoul?

▶ _____

2 Where in Seoul does the man recommend the woman to go?

▶ _____

3 What is the final place the man recommends?

▶ _____

Andrew Carnegie
"Captain of the American Steel Industry"

Industrialist and philanthropist Andrew Carnegie was born on November 25, 1835, in Dunfermline, Scotland, and was the son of a linen weaver, William Carnegie. He was not so lucky when it came to getting a formal education, but he [1] **grew up** to be one of the wealthiest businessmen in America due to his family believing in the importance of learning.

At the age of 13, Carnegie and his family moved to the United States. When he became the superintendent of the western division of the Pennsylvania Railroad, he began to make investments which brought him substantial [3] **returns**. By the late 1860s, he had become a self-made man. In the next decade, he dedicated his time to his steel company, which became known as the Carnegie Steel Company, the largest of its kind in the world. In 1901, Carnegie made a dramatic change in his life and sold his business to the United States Steel Corporation, started by legendary financier J. P. Morgan.

At the age of 65, Carnegie decided to spend the rest of his life helping others. He made numerous donations. His devotion to learning led him to establish the Carnegie Institute of Technology in Pittsburgh and the Carnegie Foundation for the Advancement of Teaching. Carnegie [2] **died of** pneumonia on August 11, 1919, with a fortune of $150 million left to his family, as well as several books, numerous articles he had written, and donations of $350 million to charities, and educational institutions.

앤드류 카네기 — "미국 철강 산업의 리더"

기업인이자 자선가인 앤드류 카네기는 1835년 11월 25일, 스코틀랜드 던펌린에서 수직공인 윌리엄 카네기의 아들로 태어났다. 그는 정규 교육을 받을 형편은 아니었지만, 배움의 중요성을 믿는 가족 덕분에 미국에서 가장 부유한 사업가 중 한 명으로 성장하였다.

13세 때 카네기와 그의 가족은 미국으로 이주했다. 그는 펜실베니아 철도회사의 서부 구역 감독이 되었을 때 투자를 하기 시작했는데, 이 투자가 그에게 상당한 이윤을 안겨주었고, 1860년대 말에는 그로 인해 자수성가하게 되었다. 그 후 10년간, 그는 철강 회사에 자신의 인생을 바쳤으며 철강업계에서는 세계적으로 가장 큰 규모의 카네기 철강 회사로 이름을 알리게 되었다. 1901년, 카네기는 자신의 기업을 전설적인 금융업자인 J.P. 모건이 설립한 US 스틸 사에 매도하면서 인생의 극적인 전환점을 맞는다.

65세의 나이에, 카네기는 자신의 남은 생을 다른 사람들을 도우며 보내기로 결심한다. 그는 수많은 기부를 하고 교육에 대한 남다른 열정으로 피츠버그에 카네기 공과대학과 카네기 교육진흥재단을 설립했다. 카네기는 1919년 8월 11일, 폐렴으로 사망했으며, 그가 집필한 수 권의 책, 그리고 수많은 논설과 함께 자신의 재산 1억5천만 달러를 그의 가족에게 남기고, 기부금 3억5천만 달러는 자선단체와 교육기관에 기부하였다.

1 grow up 성장하다, 발전하다

▶ grow up은 육체적 또는 정신적 성숙 모두를 일컫는 표현으로, grow up to be 혹은 grow into someone[something]이라고 하면 '~으로 성장하다, ~이 되다'라는 의미가 된다.

He **grew up** to be a famous painter.
그는 어른이 되어 유명한 화가가 되었다.

2 die of ~로 죽다

▶ die 뒤에 원인이 뒤따라올 때 사고나 질병과 같은 물리적인 원인일 때는 from을, 질병과 같은 자연적인 원인일 때는 of를 쓴다.

She **died** suddenly of heart failure.
그녀는 심장 마비로 급사하였다.
The slaves **died from** hard work and hunger.
그 노예들은 중노동과 굶주림으로 죽었다.

3 return 보답, 수익

The **return** on the money we invested was very low.
우리가 투자했던 그 돈의 수익은 매우 적었다.

4 leave a fortune to ~에게 재산을 남기다

▶ fortune은 '운(chance), 운명(fate)'이라는 의미로도 많이 쓰이지만 여기서는 '많은 재산'을 의미한다.

He **left a fortune** of more than 200 million dollars **to** his descendents.
그는 후손들에게 2억 달러가 넘는 재산을 남겼다.

A Carnegie library

Who is Andrew Carnegie?

미국 최고의 기업가이자 자선사업가. 1835년에 스코틀랜드에서 가난한 직조공의 아들로 태어나 방적공부터 기관 조수, 전보 배달원, 전신기사 등 여러 가지 직업을 거쳤다. 1953년에 펜실베니아 철도에 입사하고 철도건설 자재 공급에 관심을 가져 제철업에 진출하였다. 남북전쟁 이후에는 철광업을 시작하여 10년이 채 되기도 전에 미국 최대철강회사로 키워냈다. 그 후 1901년에 기업을 매각하고 은퇴하였다. 그 뒤 18년 동안 '부는 신으로부터 맡겨진 것'이라는 신념 아래 막대한 재산을 교육, 문화, 과학과 기술 재단에 기부하는 데 힘썼다. 또한, 그는 사업과 사회 본연의 자세를 설파하는 저술 활동에 전념하면서 여생을 보냈다.

Andrew Carnegie Says...

"The best way to predict the future is to create it."
미래를 예측하는 최고의 방법은 그것을 창조하는 것입니다.

"Management is doing things right; leadership is doing the right things."
관리는 일을 올바르게 하게끔 하는 것이고, 리더십은 올바른(해야 할) 일을 하는 것입니다.

"No person will make a great business who wants to do it all himself or get all the credit."
모든 일을 혼자서 하거나 모든 공로를 혼자서만 인정받기를 바라는 사람은 성공할 수 없습니다.

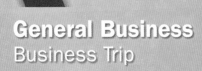

General Business
Business Trip

PART 4
해외 출장

공항 이용하기

Using the Airport

Vocabulary & Expressions

항공 예약 및 탑승 수속 Booking a Flight & Checking in

- **economy class** 일반석 **business class** 비즈니스석 **first class** 일등석
- **one-way ticket** 편도 티켓 **round-trip ticket** 왕복 티켓
- **return ticket** 돌아오는 비행편을 위한 티켓
- **direct flight** 직행 항공편 (= nonstop flight)
- **flight number** 항공편 번호
- **departure time** 출발 시간 **arrival time** 도착 시간
- **connecting flight** 연결 항공편
- **reservation number** 예약 번호
- **window seat** 창가 좌석 **aisle seat** 통로 쪽 좌석

- **legroom** 다리를 뻗을 수 있는 공간
- **carry-on luggage** 기내에 들고 탈 수 있는 짐
- **boarding pass** 탑승권
- **book a flight** 항공편을 예약하다 (= reserve a flight)
- **check in** 탑승 수속하다
- **transfer** 갈아타다

입국 심사 & 세관 Immigration & Customs

- **check-in (counter)** 체크인 카운터
- **luggage** 수하물, 짐 (= baggage)
- **security check** 보안 검사
- **passport control** 출입국 관리
- **baggage claim** 수하물 찾는 곳
- **purpose of visit** 방문 목적
- **customs declaration form** 세관 신고서
- **final destination** 최종 목적지
- **prohibited items** 금지 품목
- **fill out the form** 양식을 작성하다 (= complete the form)
- **declare** 신고하다

🔄 환전

- exchange 환전하다
- traveler's check 여행자 수표
- cash 소액 동전
- currency exchange booth 환전소
- exchange rate 환율
- money-changing machine 환전기

Useful Expressions

I'd like to book a ticket to San Francisco, please.	샌프란시스코행 티켓을 예약하고 싶습니다.
I'm calling to confirm my reservation.	예약을 확인하고 싶어서 전화했습니다.
Would you like a window seat or an aisle seat?	창가 자리와 통로 쪽 자리 중 어디가 좋으십니까?
I will be transferring in Hong Kong.	홍콩에서 갈아탈 겁니다.
I have two bags to check in .	수속할 가방이 2개 있습니다.

Vocabulary Check-Up

A Match the meanings on the left with the expressions on the right.

1 통로 쪽 좌석 · · ⓐ aisle seat

2 탑승권 · · ⓑ customs declaration form

3 세관 신고서 · · ⓒ baggage claim

4 수하물 찾는 곳 · · ⓓ prohibited items

5 금지 품목 · · ⓔ boarding pass

B Fill in the blanks with the given words.

1 다음 주 뉴욕행 항공편 예약을 확인하려고 전화했습니다.

▶ I'm calling to _____ _____ _____ for a flight to New York next week.

2 LA행 티켓을 예약하고 싶습니다.

▶ I'd like to _____ _____ _____ to LA, please.

3 매표소에서 제 짐을 수속하려고 기다리는 중입니다.

▶ I am waiting to _____ my luggage _____ at the ticket window.

4 기다리시는 동안, 이 양식을 작성하셔도 됩니다.

▶ While you are waiting, you can _____ _____ this form, sir.

> **Words**
> check in
> book a ticket
> fill out
> confirm one's reservation

C Refer to the Korean and fill in the blanks.

1 I would prefer to have a _____ _____. 창가 자리가 좋을 것 같군요.

2 Would you give me a _____ _____, please? 돌아오는 항공 티켓을 주시겠습니까?

3 Do you want a one-way or a _____ _____? 편도랑 왕복 티켓 중 어느 걸 원하세요?

4 Can I have a seat with more _____? 다리를 뻗을 수 있는 공간이 있는 좌석을 주시겠어요?

5 Do you have any _____ _____, sir? 비행기 안에 들고 탈 짐이 있으신가요?

Do you have anything to declare? 신고하실 게 있습니까?

You should fill out the form. 양식을 작성하셔야 합니다.

My bags haven't arrived yet. 제 가방이 아직 도착하지 않았어요.

How long are you staying? 얼마 동안 머무실 건가요?

Is there any place you can stay while you're visiting Paris? 파리를 방문하는 동안 계실 곳이 있나요?

44.mp3

A ¹**May I have your** ticket, **please**?

B Here you go.

A KAL Flight 730 to London.

B Yes, that's right.

A Do you have any luggage to check, Mr. Kim?

B Yes, I do. ²**I'd like to check** these two, please.

A Okay. ³**Would you prefer** a window seat **or** an aisle seat?

B I'd prefer to have a window seat.

A I can give you seat 35B. Here's your boarding pass.

Pattern Training

1 **May I have your** _____, **please?** (당신의) ~을 보여주시겠어요?

① passport
② reservation number
③ identification

▶ 여권 / 예약 번호 / 신분증

2 **I'd like to check** _____. ~을 수속하고 싶습니다.

① one bag
② two suitcases
③ two bags and my golf clubs

▶ 가방 한 개 / 여행가방 두 개 / 가방 두 개와 골프채 세트

3 **Would you prefer** _____ **or** _____?
~을 선호하십니까, 아니면 …을 선호하십니까?

① a coffee, a tea
② a turkey, a tuna sandwich
③ a beer, an orange juice

▶ 커피, 차 / 칠면조 샌드위치, 참치 샌드위치 / 맥주, 오렌지 주스

45.mp3

A May I see your passport?

B Yes, certainly.

A [1]**What's the purpose of** your visit?

B I'm going on a business trip.

A [2]**How long** are you planning to stay in London?

B About a week.

A [3]**Where will you** be staying?

B I'll be staying at the GK Hotel.

A Okay. Have a good visit.

B Thanks.

Pattern Training

1 **What's the purpose of** [_____]**?** ~의 목적이 무엇입니까?

① your trip
② your stay
③ the meeting

▶ 여행 / 체류 / 회의

2 **How long** [_____]**?** 얼마나 오래 ~?

① does it take
② will you be staying
③ will it take to get there

▶ 걸립니까 / 머물 겁니까 / 거기에 도착하는 데 걸립니까

3 **Where will you** [_____]**?** 어디에서 ~할 겁니까?

① spend your vacation
② be flying in from
③ go after the meeting

▶ 휴가를 보낼 / 비행기를 타고 오실 / 회의 후에 (어디에) 가실

Practice 1 | Let's Speak!

A Find the correct responses to complete the dialogs.

1 Do you have anything to declare?
2 Your passport, please.
3 My suitcase hasn't arrived yet.
4 Your bag is overweight.
5 I'd like to change some money. I have Korean won. Do you have pounds?
6 How would you like it, sir? In traveler's checks or cash?

Answers

ⓐ How much is the excess baggage fee?
ⓑ Please fill out this form and describe your bag.
ⓒ No, I don't have anything except my personal belongings.
ⓓ Here you are.
ⓔ Could I have $1,000 in traveler's checks and $500 in cash, please?
ⓕ Sure, we do. How much are you changing, sir?

B Complete the short dialogs.

1

A: May I help you?
B: I'd like to _____.
(예약한 비행편을 확인하고 싶습니다.)
A: Can I _____, please?
(성함과 도착지를 말씀해 주세요.)
B: My name is David Clinton, and my destination is Texas, in the U.S.

2

A: _____?(방문 목적이 무엇입니까?)
B: I'm going sightseeing.
A: _____ in Seattle?(시애틀에 얼마나 머무실 계획입니까?)
B: About two weeks.
A: _____?(어디에 머무실 겁니까?)
B: I'll be staying at the Paradise Hotel.
A: Okay. Have a good visit!

A Listen to the dialog and check true or false.   46.mp3

	True	False
1 This conversation takes place in a souvenir shop.		
2 The man wants to change Korean won into dollars.		
3 There's no fee for exchanging money.		
4 The man wants about $1,000 in cash.		

B Listen again and complete the blanks.   46.mp3

Client: I'd like to exchange some Korean won for dollars.

Changer: Okay. ¹_____ _____ _____ _____, sir?

Client: I need about $1,500. ²_____ _____ _____ _____?

Changer: It's 1,290 won per dollar. And there's a 1 percent fee.

Client: I see.

Changer: ³_____ _____ _____ your money, sir?

Client: ⁴_____ _____ _____ $1,000 in cash, please?

Changer: Certainly. Please wait a moment.

Money Exchange

C Listen to the dialog and number the sentences in order.   47.mp3

(　) Yes, I had my name, address, and even my phone number on it.

(　) Excuse me. My suitcase hasn't arrived yet.

(　) I see. Did you have your name on your name tag?

(　) Could you give me a minute so that I can look for it?

(　) I've been waiting at least an hour at the luggage carousel, but I still haven't seen my bags.

Q: What's the woman's problem?

▶ _____

WEEK 11

교통수단 이용하기

Using Transportation

Vocabulary & Expressions

길 물어보기 Asking Directions

- **direction** 방향, 위치
- **near here** 이 근처에
- **opposite** ~의 맞은편에
- **across from** ~의 건너편에
- **beside** ~ 옆에 (= next to)
- **in front of** ~ 앞에
- **behind** ~ 뒤에
- **at the corner of** ~의 모퉁이에
- **on one's right** ~의 오른쪽에 (on one's left ~의 왼쪽에)
- **within walking distance** 걸어갈 수 있는 거리에
- **map** 지도 **landmark** 대표 건물, 명소
- **overpass** 가로지르다
- **get to** ~에 가다, 도착하다

🔊 지하철·버스·택시 이용하기

- **Take me to [장소].**
  [장소]로 가주세요.
- **get on / get off**
  (전철·버스 등의 큰 교통수단을) 타다/내리다
- **get in / get out**
  (승용차·택시 등의 작은 교통수단을) 타다/내리다
- **transfer to ... heading to ~**
  ~행 …으로 갈아타다

- **look for** ~을 찾다
- **go straight along the street** 길을 따라 직진하다
- **turn left** 왼쪽으로 꺾다
- **go up (street name)** (~길을) 따라 올라가다

자동차 렌트하기 Renting a Car

- **compact car** 소형차 (= economy car)
- **rent-a-car company** 렌터카 회사 (= car rental company)
- **rental rate** 렌트 요금
- **date of return** 반납일
- **dent** 움푹 들어간 곳 **scratch** 흠집 **damage** 손상
- **highway, freeway, expressway** 고속도로
- **automatic transmission** 자동 변속장치

- **gas tank** 연료 탱크 (= fuel tank)
- **deposit** 보증금
- **driver's license** 운전 면허증
- **insurance** 보험
- **gas station** 주유소
- **comprehensive coverage** 종합 보험
- **manual (car)** 수동변속 차량

Useful Expressions

Can you tell me how to get there ?

거기 가는 **방법을** 알려 주시겠어요?

Go past the post office, and then you will see Chestnut Street.

우체국을 **지나서 가세요**. 그러면 체스넛 거리가 **보일 겁니다**.

Where is the nearest subway station?

가장 가까운 지하철역이 어디입니까?

Please drop me off near the subway station.

지하철역 근처에 **내려주세요**.

I'd like to rent a car, please.

차를 빌리고 싶습니다.

A Match the meanings on the left with the expressions on the right.

1 버스 정류장 ·   · ⓐ automatic transmission

2 방향, 위치 ·   · ⓑ bus stop

3 소형차 ·   · ⓒ compact car

4 종합 보험 ·   · ⓓ direction

5 자동 변속장치 ·   · ⓔ comprehensive coverage

B Fill in the blanks with the given words.

1 이 길을 따라 직진하다 보면 우측에 백화점이 있을 거예요.

▶ _____ _____ along this street, and you will see the department store on your right.

2 여기서 멀지 않아요. 메인 가를 내려가다가, 프레몬트 가에서 왼쪽으로 도세요.

▶ It's not far from here; _____ _____ Main Street, and _____ _____ on Fremont Street.

3 메트로폴리탄 박물관에 가려면 어느 역에서 내려야 합니까?

▶ Which station should I _____ _____ at to get to the Metropolitan Museum?

4 3일간 차를 빌리기로 예약했습니다.

▶ I have a car _____ for 3 days.

> Words
> reserve
> turn left
> get off
> go straight
> go down

C Refer to the Korean and fill in the blanks.

1 The restaurant is _____ _____ the department store. 그 식당은 백화점 건너편에 있습니다.

2 Please _____ _____ somewhere that I can find a Thai restaurant. 태국식 식당이 있는 곳으로 가주세요.

3 Is there a bank _____ _____? 이 근처에 은행이 있나요?

4 I'd like to _____ _____ _____. 차를 반납하고 싶습니다.

5 Take the yellow line to Chinatown, and then _____ _____ the red line.

노란색 노선을 타고 차이나타운까지 가서, 빨간색 노선으로 갈아타세요.

What kind of cars do you have?   어떤 종류의 차가 있습니까?

How long would you like to rent it for?   얼마 동안 렌트하실 건가요?

Does that include insurance?   거기에 보험료도 포함됩니까?

How much is the rental rate?   렌트 요금은 얼마입니까?

I have a car reserved for 3 days.   3일간 차를 빌리기로 예약해 두었습니다.

48.mp3

A **¹Can you tell me how to get to** the Twin Tower Building?

B Yes, you go straight along this street and take the third left. Then go up the street **²until you see a hospital**. Go around the corner on your left, and you will see the Twin Tower Building on your right.

A Thank you, but **³is there an easier way to** get there?

B You can take a taxi, but it's within walking distance.

A Okay, is there some sort of a landmark you can tell me about?

B Yes, Seoul City Hall is around there. It's right next to the Twin Tower Building.

Pattern Training \

1 **Can you tell me how to get to** [_____]**?** ~로 가는 방법을 말씀해 주시겠어요?

① the convention center
② 1st Avenue
③ the subway station near here

▶ 컨벤션 센터 / 1번가 / 이 근처의 지하철역

🚕 택시 기사에게 목적지 말하기

- Driver: Where would you like to go?
  어디로 가시겠습니까?
- Customer:
  I'd like to go to *Gwanghwamun*.
  = **Could you take me to**
    Gwanghwamun, **please?**
  = *Gwanghwamun*, **please**.
    광화문으로 가 주세요.

2 [_____] **until you see a hospital.**
병원이 보일 때까지 ~하세요.

① Go straight
② Go down the street
③ Drive down the road

▶ 직진하세요 / 길을 내려가세요 / 도로를 따라 운전해 내려가세요

3 **Is there an easier way to** [_____]**?** ~하는 더 쉬운 방법이 있나요?

① get to the hotel
② arrive at the museum by public transportation
③ reach the park

▶ 호텔에 가는 / 대중교통으로 박물관에 도착하는 / 공원에 가는

Conversation 2 | Renting a Car 자동차 렌트하기

49.mp3

A I'd like to rent a car, please.

B **[1]Do you have any particular** brand of car **in mind**?

A No, but I'm looking for a compact car.

B Okay. Let me see what we've got left. We have a Chevrolet Cobalt.

A How much is the rental rate?

B It's $100 per day. That includes insurance. **[2]How long would you like to** rent it for?

A I'll need it for three days. **[3]What does** the insurance **cover**?

B It's comprehensive coverage. Can I have your driver's license, please?

A Certainly. Here you are.

Pattern Training

1 **Do you have any particular** [_____] **in mind?**
마음에 두고 있는 특별한 ~가 있나요?

① color
② design
③ kind

▶ 색상 / 디자인 / 종류

2 **How long would you like to** [_____]**?** 얼마 동안 ~하기를 원하십니까?

① use it
② stay there
③ travel for

▶ 그것을 사용하기를 / 거기에 머물기를 / 여행하기를

3 **What does** [_____] **cover?** ~이 어디까지 포함하고 있습니까?

① the test
② the policy
③ the history book

▶ 시험(시험 범위를 물어볼 때) / 정책 / 역사책

Practice 1 / Let's Speak!

A Find the correct responses to complete the dialogs.

1 Can you tell me how to get to the department store?
2 Is there some sort of a landmark you can tell me about?
3 Where would you like to go?
4 Do you have any particular car in mind?
5 What does the insurance cover?
6 Is there an easier way to get there?

Answers
ⓐ Yes, you go straight along this street and take the third left. You will see it on your left.
ⓑ There's no fast way during rush hour.
ⓒ Yes, the GT department store is around there.
ⓓ Gwanghwamun, please.
ⓔ I'm looking for a compact car.
ⓕ It's comprehensive coverage.

B Complete the short dialogs.

1

A: Excuse me. _____ to go to the Twin Tower Building?(Twin Tower로 가려면 어느 버스를 타야 하죠?)

B: Take bus number 600.

A: _____ from here to the Twin Tower Building?
(여기서 Twin Tower까지 몇 정거장을 가야 하죠?)

B: You can _____.(세 번째 정거장에서 하차하세요.)

2

A: Excuse me, but _____

the Kennedy Center?(케네디 센터에 가는 방법을 알려 주실 수 있으세요?)

B: Certainly. Go straight _____.

(두 번째 신호등이 보일 때까지 계속 가세요.) And then _____

to Oak Street.(그러고 나서 왼쪽으로 돌아서 오크 가로 두 블록 걸어가세요.)

A: Thank you very much.

A Listen to the dialog and answer the questions.

50.mp3

1 What kind of car did the woman finally rent?

▶

2 What did the woman hand out to the man?

▶

3 What sort of insurance did you woman choose?

▶

4 What is the daily rental rate including tax?

▶

B Listen again and complete the blanks.

50.mp3

Customer: I'd like to __¹____ ____ ____.

Assistant: What type of car would you like?

Customer: I want an economy car.

Assistant: I'm sorry, but __²____ ____ ____ ____ ____ ____ now.

Customer: Then, I'll take a mid-sized car.

Assistant: All right. __³____ ____ ____ your driver's license and credit card?

Customer: Here you are. __⁴____ ____ ____ ____ ____?

Assistant: It's 26 dollars a day plus tax. Would you like to buy optional insurance?

Customer: No, __⁵____ ____ ____ ____.

+ BIZ TIPs 여러 나라의 교통카드

해외 출장을 갔을 때, 지하철이나 버스를 탈 때마다 표를 사게 되면 비싸고 번거로우므로 일일 승차권을 사거나, 이틀 이상 머무는 경우엔 지하철이나 버스, 철도를 모두 이용할 수 있는 교통카드를 이용하는 것이 좋다. 뉴욕에는 한국 T-money(교통카드)와 비슷한 개념인 MetroCard가 있으며 영국의 런던에는 Oyster 카드, 홍콩에는 Octopus 카드가 있다. 지하철(subway)을 가리키는 말도 나라마다 약간씩 다른데, 미국에서는 metro, 영국에서는 underground 또는 tube라고 한다.

무역박람회 참가하기

Attending a Trade Show

Vocabulary & Expressions

무역 박람회 At the Trade Show

- **ID card** 신분증
- **participant** 참가자
- **presenter** 발표자
- **registration** 접수, 등록 (register for ~에 등록하다)
- **as part of** ~의 한 부분으로, 일환으로
- **free of charge** 무료로
- **booth** (전시장의) 부스
- **catalog** 카탈로그
- **pamphlet** 팜플렛, 소책자
- **attend** 참석하다
- **be on display** ~가 전시되다 (= be displayed)
- **run** 진행하다, 운영하다 (= operate)

🔊 비즈니스 행사

- **exhibition / fair / show**
  전시회, 박람회 (*용어에 따라 약간의 규모 차이가 있다)
- **convention** 집회, 모임
- **conference** 회의
- **seminar** 세미나
- **presentation** 설명회

- **display** 전시하다 (= exhibit)
- **exhibit** 전시물, 전시품; 전시하다
- **send out an invitation** 초대장을 발송하다

제품 소개 Product Introduction

- **product's features** 제품의 특징
- **selling point** (판매시) 상품의 강점
- **key functions** (제품의) 주요 기능
- **suitable[ideal, perfect] for** ~에 적합한
- **specification** 제품 사양 (= spec)
- **prototype** 표본, 견본
- **high demand** 높은 수요

- **durability** 내구성 **resilience** 복원력
- **launch** 출시하다 **release** 출시
- **under warranty[guarantee]** 보증 기간 중인
- **meet customers' needs** 소비자를 만족시키다
- **place an order** 주문하다
- **quote** 거래 가격
- **unit price** 단가

Useful Expressions

The New York trade show will be held this September.	뉴욕 무역박람회가 오는 9월에 열립니다.
Please drop by our booth and pick up a free sample.	저희 부스에 들러서 무료 샘플을 가져가세요.
Could you show me how it works?	어떻게 작동하는지 보여주시겠어요?
What are the specifications of the product?	그 제품의 **사양은 어떻게** 됩니까?
Would it be possible to get a brochure?	브로셔를 받을 수 있을까요?

A Match the meanings on the left with the expressions on the right.

1 등록하다 ·   · ⓐ participant

2 참가자 ·   · ⓑ exhibit

3 전시물 ·   · ⓒ register

4 상품의 강조점 ·   · ⓓ specifications

5 제품 사양 ·   · ⓔ selling point

B Fill in the blanks with the given words.

1 여분의 브로셔를 몇 개 가져가도 될까요?

  ▶ Would it be possible to get some _____ _____?

2 그 제품의 이점은 무엇입니까?

  ▶ What are the product's _____?

3 젊은 소비층에게 그 제품에 대한 수요가 높습니다.

  ▶ There's a _____ _____ for the product among young consumers.

4 새로 개발된 저희 제품을 보여드리고 싶습니다.

  ▶ I guess you'd like to see our _____ _____ product.

> **Words**
> brochures
> benefits
> high demand
> extra
> newly developed

C Refer to the Korean and fill in the blanks.

1 Could you _____ _____ how to work this gadget? 이 장치를 작동시키는 법을 보여주시겠습니까?

2 This product comes _____ a 2-year _____. 이 제품은 2년간의 품질보증이 따라옵니다.

3 The low labor cost is one of the biggest _____ _____ of this product.

  인건비가 적게 든다는 것이 이 제품을 판매 시 가장 큰 강점이 됩니다.

4 Let me _____ you _____ _____ about this product. 이 제품에 관한 몇 가지 정보를 드리겠습니다.

5 Any questions? I'll be happy to _____ _____ _____ you may have.

  질문 있으십니까? 어떤 질문이라도 기꺼이 답변해 드리겠습니다.

Can you tell me what this device is for ?   이 장치의 용도가 무엇인지 말씀해 주시겠습니까?

Let me give you some information about this product.   이 제품에 대해 몇 가지 설명을 드리겠습니다.

I'll be happy to answer any questions you may have .   어떤 질문이라도 기쁘게 답변 드리겠습니다.

One of the advantages of this product is that it's easy to use.   이 제품의 장점 중 하나는 사용하기가 편하다는 겁니다.

Compared with other products , ours is easier to operate.   다른 제품들에 비해 저희 제품은 조작이 간편합니다.

51.mp3

A ¹**I'm here for the convention, as** a visitor.

B Okay. Can I have your ID, please? Every visitor has to be registered.

A Certainly. Here you are.

B Okay… Here's your ID back. We have our welcoming pack in this bag. In the welcoming pack, ²**there should be** a map of the hall **so** you can find your way. There is also a list of the participating companies and information about them.

A Thank you. ³**Would it be possible to** get some extra brochures? I want to share them with my colleagues.

B Sure, here you are, sir. If you need any help, please let me know.

Pattern Training \

1 **I'm here for the convention, as** [＿＿＿＿＿＿]. 회의에 ~(자격)으로 왔습니다.

① an exhibitor
② a presenter
③ a participant

▶ 전시자 / 발표자 / 참석자

2 **There should be** [＿＿＿＿＿] **so** [＿＿＿＿＿].
~이 있을 테니 …할 겁니다.

① a contact number and address on my business card, you can contact me when you need to
② all the information you need in my email, you will know what's going on
③ a gift certificate as a present to you in the envelope, you can celebrate your birthday

▶ 제 명함에 연락처와 주소가 있을 테니 필요하실 때 연락 주십시오 / 제 전자메일에 필요로 하신 모든 정보가 있을 테니 무슨 일인지 아시게 될 겁니다 / 봉투 안에 당신께 드리는 선물인 상품권이 있을 테니 생일을 즐겁게 보내세요

3 **Would it be possible to** [＿＿＿＿＿]? ~하는 것이 가능할까요?

① use a projector during my presentation
② get into the conference without registration
③ reserve seats in advance

▶ 프레젠테이션 중에 프로젝터를 사용하는 것 / 등록하지 않고 회의장에 입실하는 것 / 미리 좌석을 예약하는 것

52.mp3

A ¹**Can you tell me** what the device is for?

B This is what we call a little giant. It looks just like a regular battery. But ²**the best thing about our product is that** it can be used for a month without recharging.

A How long is the warranty?

B This product comes with a 2-year warranty.

A ³**Could you show me how to** adapt this device to my cell phone again?

B Okay. It's easy. I'd be happy to show you again.

Pattern Training

1 **Can you tell me** [＿＿＿＿＿]?
~을 말씀해 주시겠어요?

① what you know about this gadget
② how to work this device
③ why prices go up and down

▶ 이 기계에 대해 아는 것 / 이 장치를 작동시키는 방법 / 가격이 오르락내리락 하는 이유

🔊 제품에 대한 설명 요청

· Could you tell me a little about the **functions**?
기능에 대해서 좀 말씀해 주시겠어요?

· Can you tell me about its **features**?
특징을 말씀해 주시겠어요?

· Can you tell me about its **use[application]**?
용도[활용]에 대해서 말씀해 주시겠어요?

2 **The best thing about our product is that** [＿＿＿＿＿].
저희 제품의 최대 장점은 ~라는 점입니다.

① it is waterproof
② it comes with a 10-year warranty
③ it is much cheaper than the previous model

▶ 방수 제품이다 / 10년 동안 보증이 된다 / 이전 모델보다 훨씬 가격이 싸다

3 **Could you show me how to** [＿＿＿＿＿]? 어떻게 ~하는지 좀 보여주시겠습니까?

① use this program
② operate the machine
③ turn this off

▶ 이 프로그램을 어떻게 사용하는지 / 그 기계를 어떻게 작동시키는지 / 이것을 어떻게 끄는지

Practice 1 — Let's Speak!

A Find the correct responses to complete the dialogs.

1 I'd like to learn a little bit more about your product.
2 What are the advantages of this device?
3 Are there any new features compared to the previous models?
4 When it comes to software, we're more quality-conscious.
5 Can I have a look at a demo?

Answers
ⓐ One of the major advantages is that it is energy-efficient.
ⓑ Please look at page ten of the catalog. It can give you a better explanation.
ⓒ The latest model is equipped with a small camera.
ⓓ Sure. And you can take this free trial of our software.
ⓔ If so, I'm sure that you'll be satisfied with this software.

B Complete the short dialogs.

1

A: _____.(이것이 저희 새 모델입니다.) The most advanced technology has been applied.

B: Are there any features different from the last type?

A: We're sure that it is _____.
(경쟁사들에 비해 더 경제적이고 효율적이라고 확신합니다.)

B: I see. _____?(어떻게 작동하는지 보여주시겠어요?)

A: Sure.

2

A: Can you tell me _____?(이 장치의 용도가 뭔지 말씀해 주실래요?)

B: It can recharge any product with batteries.

A: What are its advantages?

B: _____ it is designed to conserve energy.(이 제품의 이점 중 하나는 에너지가 절약되도록 설계됐다는 점입니다.)

A: Would it _____?(브로셔를 하나 가져가도 될까요?)

B: Sure. I've got some right here.

Practice 2 — Listen-up!

A · Listen to the dialog and check true or false.

53.mp3

	True	False
1 The man registered onsite to visit the trade show.		
2 The man received a bag with some demo CDs and catalogs.		
3 Visitors shouldn't take any pictures at the exhibition.		
4 The man should wear his name tag at the trade show.		

B · Listen again and complete the blanks.

53.mp3

Receptionist: Good morning.

Visitor: Good morning. ¹_____ _____, and this is my confirmation slip.

Receptionist: Let me see. You're Mr. Steven Johnson?

Visitor: Yes, I am.

Receptionist: Okay. ²_____ ____ _____ _____ _____. Please ³_____ _____ _____ _____ _____ in the trade show hall.

Visitor: I will.

Receptionist: Here's our welcoming bag. The map of the hall, the show program, ⁴_____ _____ ____ _____, _____ _____ _____... They're all in it.

Visitor: Thank you. ⁵_____ ____ _____ _____ at the exhibition?

Receptionist: In principle, no. But some of the exhibitors may let you. ⁶_____ _____ _____ _____ at each booth.

호텔과 레스토랑 이용하기

Using Hotels and Restaurants

Vocabulary & Expressions

호텔 이용하기 Using Hotels

- **vacancy** 빈방
- **a room available** 이용 가능한 방
- **be all booked** 예약이 다 차다 (= be fully booked)
- **check in** 투숙 절차를 밟다, 체크인하다
- **have a reservation** 예약해 두다
- **amenities** (호텔 등의) 편의시설
- **room rate** 객실 요금
- **pay by[with] Visa** 비자 카드로 계산하다
- **accept[take] MasterCard** 마스터 카드를 받다
- **swipe the credit card** 신용카드를 판독기에 긁다(신용카드로 계산하다)
- **check out** 체크아웃하다

방의 종류

- single room 1인실   double room 2인실
- twin room 트윈 룸(침대가 두 개인 객실)
- smoking room 흡연실   nonsmoking room 금연실
- a room with an ocean view 바다가 보이는 방

- **hotel courtesy bus** 호텔 셔틀 버스
- **wake-up call** 모닝콜 (전화로 손님을 깨워주는 서비스)
- **room service** 룸 서비스 (객실로 가져다주는 서비스)
- **complimentary dinner** 무료로 주는 석식

레스토랑 이용하기 Using Restaurants

- **reserve a table for two** 2명 자리를 예약하다
- **regular customer** 단골 손님
- **today's specials** 오늘의 특별요리
- **recommend** 추천하다
- **starter** 전채요리 (= appetizer)
- **main dish** 주요리 (= entrée)
- **rare** 덜 익힌   **medium rare** 약간 덜 익힌   **medium** 중간 정도 익힌   **medium well** 중간보다 더 익힌   **well-done** 잘 익힌

- **be popular with[among]** ~에게 인기가 있다
- **run out of** ~가 다 떨어지다
- **be ready to order** 주문할 준비가 되다
- **have a look at the menu** 메뉴를 훑어보다
- **on the house** 식당에서 서비스로 제공하는
- **party** 일행

Useful Expressions

How long would you like to stay?

I'm sorry, but we're all booked for the weekend.

I have a room reservation for tonight.

Can you recommend a good Chinese restaurant?

Could you reserve a table for two for dinner?

얼마나 머무실 겁니까?

죄송합니다만, 주말엔 **예약이 다 찼습니다.**

오늘 묵을 **방을 예약해 두었습니다.**

괜찮은 중국 음식점을 **추천해 주시겠어요?**

저녁식사를 위해 두 명 **자리를 예약해 주시겠습니까?**

A Match the meanings on the left with the expressions on the right.

1 2인실 · · ⓐ laundry room

2 금연실 · · ⓑ complimentary dinner

3 주요리 · · ⓒ main dish

4 세탁실 · · ⓓ double room

5 무료 석식 · · ⓔ nonsmoking room

B Fill in the blanks with the given words.

1 체크인하려고요.

▶ I'd like to _____ _____.

2 1인실로 하시겠습니까, 2인실로 하시겠습니까?

▶ Would you like a _____ or a _____ room?

3 오늘 묵을 수 있는 방이 있나요?

▶ Do you have any _____ today?

4 신용카드로 계산할 수 있습니까? 비자카드 받나요?

▶ Can I _____ _____ my credit card? Do you _____ _____?

Words

check in
pay with
single
vacancies
double
take Visa

C Refer to the Korean and fill in the blanks.

1 What is the _____ _____? 객실 요금은 얼마입니까?

2 Are you _____ to order? 주문하시겠습니까?

3 I'll have the pesto bread as an _____, please. 전채요리는 페스토 빵으로 하겠습니다.

4 _____ would you _____ your steak? 스테이크를 어떻게 요리해 드릴까요?

5 I _____ the ribeye steak. 립아이 스테이크를 추천해 드립니다.

What time is breakfast served in the morning?   조식은 아침 몇 시에 나옵니까?

How much will it cost if I use your limousine service?   리무진 서비스를 이용하면 요금이 얼마나 들까요?

Are you ready to order? / May I take your order ?   주문하시겠습니까?

How would you like your steak?   스테이크를 어떻게 요리해 드릴까요?

Does that come with a salad?   샐러드도 함께 나오나요?

A ¹**Do you have any vacancies** today?

B Yes, we do. How long are you planning to stay?

A ²**I'm planning to** stay for 4 days.

B Would you like a single or a double room?

A A double, please. And can I have a smoking room with a balcony?

B Okay. Anything else, sir?

A How much do you charge per night?

B $250.

A ³**Does that include** breakfast?

B Yes, it does. Please fill out this guest registration card.

Pattern Training

1 **Do you have any vacancies** [_____]? ~ 빈방이 있나요?

① on the 10th of July
② for the first week of December
③ during the Christmas holiday

▶ 7월 10일에 / 12월 첫째 주에 / 성탄절 연휴 동안에

2 **I'm planning to** [_____]. 저는 ~할 계획입니다.

① travel for a week
② attend a conference tomorrow
③ go to bed at 12 tonight

▶ 일주일간 여행할 / 내일 컨퍼런스에 참가할 / 오늘 밤 12시에 잠자리에 들

3 **Does that include** [_____]? 거기에 ~가 포함되나요?

① a complimentary dinner
② the charge for using the facilities
③ tax

▶ 무료 석식 / 시설 이용료 / 세금

55.mp3

A May I take your order now?

B Yes, um… What would you recommend?

A Today's special is the prime rib with a glass of house wine. We serve it for $54, which is a special price only for today.

B [1]**I'll have** today's special then.

A An excellent choice. [2]**How would you like your** steak?

B Medium well, please. And I'd like a Caesar salad.

A All right. And would you like something to drink?

B Just mineral water, please.

Pattern Training

1 **I'll have** [_____]. ~으로 주세요. (음식을 주문할 때)

① the filet mignon
② the seafood pasta
③ a glass of red wine

▶ 필레미뇽(최상급 안심) / 해물 파스타 / 레드와인 한 잔

2 **How would you like your** [_____]? ~를 어떻게 요리해 드릴까요?

① eggs
② coffee
③ lamb

▶ 계란 / 커피 / 양고기

A Find the correct responses to complete the dialogs.

1 What is the rate for a single room?
2 Are you ready to order?
3 Excuse me. We didn't order this chocolate ice cream cake.
4 Do you take Visa?
5 Do you have a room available for tonight?

Answers
ⓐ It's 80 dollars per night for a single room.
ⓑ Certainly, sir. We accept both Visa and MasterCard.
ⓒ Don't worry, ma'am. It's on the house.
ⓓ I'll have the chicken soup as an appetizer, please.
ⓔ I'm sorry, but we're all booked.

B Complete the short dialogs.

1

A: Good afternoon, ma'am. May I help you?
B: _____, please.(체크인하려고 합니다.)
A: _____, ma'am?(예약하셨나요?)
B: Yes, My name is Sandra Brown.
A: Here is your key. Would you like someone _____?
　 (가방을 들어드릴까요?)
B: Yes, please.

2

A: Hilton Hotel. How may I help you?
B: _____ for May 5.(5월 5일에 방을 예약하고 싶습니다.)
A: All right. _____ do you want?(어떤 방을 원하세요?)
B: I'd like a nonsmoking room with _____.
　 (더블 침대가 두 개 있는 금연 객실로요.)
A: How many people will be staying in the room?
B: Two adults and one child.

A ▸ Listen to the dialog and check true or false.   56.mp3

	True	False
1 This conversation takes place at a restaurant.		
2 The man has a table reserved for 7 people.		
3 Today's special comes with only a salad.		
4 The man wants his steak cooked medium rare.		

B ▸ Listen again and complete the blanks.   56.mp3

Waitress: Good evening. Do you ¹_____ _____ _____?

Guest: Yes, ²_____ _____ ____ _____ _____ for 7 o'clock.

Waitress: What's the name, sir?

Guest: It's Robert Park.

Waitress: Ah, yes. This way, please.

…

Waitress: May I ³_____ _____ _____?

Guest: What's today's special?

Waitress: Today's special is the sirloin steak. ⁴____ _____ _____ _____ _____, and
roast potatoes as well.

Guest: I'll take it, please.

Waitress: An excellent choice! ⁵_____ _____ _____ _____
your steak?

Guest: I'd like it medium rare, please.

C ▸ Listen to the dialog and answer the questions.   57.mp3

1 What does the woman ask the man?

▸ _____

2 Why does the woman want to check out later?

▸ _____

3 What time is she going to check out?

▸ _____

John D. Rockefeller
"The oil baron who was bound to be rich"

A baby who would become one of a great American industrialist and philanthropist and who founded the Standard Oil Company, the University of Chicago, and the Rockefeller Foundation was born on July 8, 1839, at a farm in Richford, N.Y.

The family moved to Cleveland, Ohio, in 1853. Rockefeller found his first job clerking in a produce commission house in his first year at college. In 1859, he [1]**established** a commission business dealing in hay, grain, meats, and other goods with a young Englishman, Clark Andrews, where he controlled office management, bookkeeping, and the building of relationships with bankers. In 1863, he built an oil refinery that soon became the largest in the area. With a few associates, he incorporated the Standard Oil Co. in 1870. He managed to place the stock of the company and its affiliates in other states under the control of a board of trustees, establishing the first major U.S. business trust company. [2]**As a result of** antitrust proceedings, he later [3]**converted** the trust into a holding company.

In the 1890s, he turned his attention to philanthropy. He founded the University of Chicago in 1892, the Rockefeller Institute for Medical Research (later Rockefeller University) in 1901, and the Rockefeller Foundation in 1913. Though he kept his personal life fairly simple and rather frugal, he [4]**donated** over $500 million in his lifetime.

Standard Oil Building,
Bowling Green,
New York City.

록펠러 ― "부자가 될 수밖에 없었던 석유왕"

후에 미국의 위대한 기업가이자 자선가가 되어 스탠더드 석유 회사와 시카고 대학교, 록펠러 재단을 설립한 한 아기가 1839년 7월 8일, 뉴욕 리치포드의 한 농가에서 태어났다.

그의 가족은 1853년에 오하이오주의 클리브랜드로 이사했다. 록펠러는 대학 1학년 때에 자신의 첫 번째 직업으로, 생산 위탁 업체에서 점원으로 일한다. 1859년, 그는 사무관리와 부기, 은행원들과의 인맥 구축을 관리할 영국 청년인 클라크 앤드루스와 함께 건초와 곡물, 육류, 그 외 물품들을 취급하는 위탁 업체를 설립했다. 1863년, 록펠러는 정유소를 세우는데, 그것이 머지않아 그 지역의 가장 큰 회사가 된다. 1870년에는 소수의 동업자들과 함께 스탠더드 석유 회사를 주식회사로 만들었다. 그는 최초의 거대한 U.S. 비즈니스 트러스트 회사를 설립함으로써, 회사와 지점의 주식을 이사진의 관리하에 놓이도록 경영하였다. 반(反)트러스트 소송의 결과로, 그는 트러스트를 지주회사로 전환하였다.

1890년대에 록펠러는 자신의 관심을 자선사업으로 돌렸다. 그는 1892년에 시카고 대학을 설립했으며, 1901년엔 록펠러 의학연구소(록펠러 대학의 전신)를, 1913년엔 록펠러 재단을 설립하였다. 비록 자기 자신의 삶은 꽤 간결하고 다소 검소하게 보냈지만, 평생 5억 달러 이상을 기증하였다.

1 establish (회사·기관 등을) 설립하다

▶ 회사의 연혁을 이야기할 때 수동형 be established in + [연도]를 활용해 창립 시기를 밝힐 수 있다.

The company was established in 1952.
그 회사는 1952년에 창립되었다.

2 as a result of ~에 대한 결과로

The sales have declined as a result of the recession.
불황의 결과로 판매가 감소되었다.

3 convert A into B A를 B로 전환하다, 변경하다

He converted the basement into the spare bedroom.
그는 지하실을 여분의 침실로 변경했다.

4 donate 기증하다

▶ 돈이나 물품 등을 기부하는 것을 의미하며, 참고로 '헌혈'은 blood donation,
'장기 기증'은 organ donation이라고 한다.

An anonymous businessman donated one million dollars to the charity.
익명의 사업가가 백만 달러를 자선단체에 기증했다.

Who is John D. Rockefeller?

미국 역사상 최초의 억만장자인 존 록펠러는 성실성과 헌신성을 몸소 보여준 증인이다. 그는 거의 무일푼으로 시작하여 스탠더드 석유 회사의 창립자가 되었으며, 후엔 록펠러 재단에 자금을 지원했던 침례교회의 영향으로 자선가가 된다. 기업의 회장직에서 물러난 후에는 1896년부터 여러 학교와 보건기구, 시 공단을 지원하는 등 자선사업에 완전히 일신하였고, 그의 사후에도 재단의 자선은 계속되고 있다.

John D. Rockefeller says...

"The person who starts out simply with the idea of getting rich won't succeed; you must have a larger ambition. There is no mystery in business success. If you do each day's task successfully and stay faithfully within these natural operations of commercial laws which I talk so much about and keep your head clear, you will come out all right."

단순히 부자가 되고 싶다는 생각으로 시작하는 사람은 성공할 수 없다; 더 큰 야망을 가져야 한다. 사업의 성공에는 비밀이 없다. 그날 그날의 업무를 성공적으로 수행하고, 수차례 이야기한 상법의 실재적인 시행범위 안에서 성실하게 머물며, 사고는 명석하게 유지한다면, 당신은 성공할 것이다.

General Business
Business E-mail

SPECIAL PART
비즈니스 이메일

첫 비즈니스 이메일 보내기

Sending a Business E-mail for the First Time

Subject	A Future Relationship ——————○ 제목
From	kje@han.com ——————○ 보내는 사람
To	stevep@free.com ——————○ 받는 사람

58.mp3

Dear Mr. Park, ——————○ 인사말(Greeting)

We were given your name by Schmidt Ltd. in Germany. My name is Jeongeun Kim, and I am in charge of my company's PR Department. I'm emailing you regarding a future relationship between my company and yours. We wish to provide you with some information on our latest equipment. Should you wish to receive further information regarding this matter, please do not hesitate to contact me at the e-mail address below.

I look forward to hearing from you. ——————○ 결구(Ending)

Sincerely yours,

Jeongeun Kim
PR Manager ——————○ 보내는 사람의 이름, 직책, 연락처 등 개인 정보 첨부
kje@han.com

제목: 앞으로의 관계
박 선생님께,
독일의 슈미츠 사로부터 귀하의 존함을 받았습니다. 제 이름은 김정은이며, 홍보부를 담당하고 있습니다. 저희 회사와 귀사와의 앞으로의 거래 관계에 관해 이메일을 드리게 됐습니다. 저희 회사의 최신 장비에 대한 정보를 제공해 드리고자 합니다. 이 건과 관련해 추가 정보를 원하시면, 주저하지 마시고 아래의 이메일 주소로 연락 주시길 바랍니다.
소식 주시길 기대하겠습니다.
친애하는,

김정은
홍보 부장
kje@han.com

Dear Mr.(Ms) + 성 ~께 담당자 이름을 모른다면 To whom it may concern, 또는 Dear Sir or Madam,이라고 하면 된다.

be in charge of ~을 담당하다 be responsible for도 같은 뜻. in charge of 다음에는 부서 또는 업무 내용이 온다.

> I **am in charge of** the new project.
> ▶ 저는 새로운 프로젝트를 담당하고 있습니다.

We wish to provide you with ~을 제공해 드리고자 합니다 'provide + 사람 + with'의 형태는 '~에게 …을 제공하다'의 의미가 된다.

> **We wish to provide you with** some information on our new products.
> ▶ 저희 신제품에 대한 정보를 제공해 드리고자 합니다.

Should you wish to do 만약 ~하고 싶으시면 이 경우의 should는 '~한다면'이라는 가정의 의미가 있는 if를 대신하고 있다.
> If 대신에 Should를 사용하면 매우 격식을 차린 표현이 된다.

> **Should you wish to** have some further information about this matter, please contact me.
> ▶ 이 건과 관련해 더 많은 정보를 원하시면 제게 연락 주십시오.

look forward to ~를 고대하다 to 다음에는 명사, 또는 동사의 -ing형이 온다.

> I'm **looking forward to** meeting you.
> ▶ 당신을 만나 뵙길 기대합니다.

Sincerely yours, 친애하는 결구(closing)에 일반적으로 쓰이는 표현

> Sincerely yours, / Sincerely, [약간 격식을 차린 표현]
> Best regards, / Regards, / With best wishes, / Best wishes, [친한 사이나 그렇지 않은 사람 모두에게 사용 가능한 표현]

Vocabulary Check-Up

Fill in the blanks with the appropriate expressions.

1 필립스 씨께(man)

> ▶ _____ _____ Philips,

2 제 이름은 조지 마이클입니다.

> ▶ _____ _____ ____ George Michael.

3 저는 연구개발부를 담당하고 있습니다.

> ▶ I am ____ _____ ____ the R&D Department.

4 담당자님 앞

> ▶ To _____ ____ _____ concern

5 답신을 기다리겠습니다.

> ▶ I _____ _____ ____ your response.

1 "~을 담당하고 있습니다" [자기소개 하기]

▶ 처음 보내는 메일에는 자신의 소개와 더불어, 회사에 대한 소개를 포함하는 것이 좋다.

> **My name is** Jeongeun Kim, and **I am in charge of** the PR Department. **Our company is** a subsidiary of MNC, and **we specialize in** pharmaceutical products. We wish to provide you with some information on our cutting edge equipment.

제 이름은 김정은이며, 홍보부를 **맡고 있습니다. 저희 회사는** MNC의 자회사로서 의약 제품을 **전문으로 다루고 있습니다.** 선생님께 저희 회사의 최첨단 장비에 대한 자료를 제공해 드리고 싶습니다.

2 "~관하여 이메일 드립니다" [이메일의 목적 밝히기]

▶ 이메일을 보내는 목적을 밝힐 때 '~와 관련하여'라는 의미로 격식을 차려 표현할 때는 regarding을 주로 쓴다.

> **I am e-mailing you regarding** your complaint dated October. 4. I assure you that the issues you raised in your email will be the first priority for us to deal with.

10월 4일에 보내주신 고객의 불만사항 **때문에 이메일 드립니다.** 귀하께서 이메일에 거론하신 문제들을 최우선으로 처리해 드릴 것을 약속드립니다.

3 "언제든 연락 주십시오" [문의 및 연락을 환영할 때]

▶ 보내는 메일에 대해 상대방이 갖게 될 의문점이나 궁금증을 해결해 주기 위해 연락 가능한 통로를 안내하는 것이 좋다.

> If you desire further information, **please do not hesitate to contact** our local office, the address and telephone number of which are given below.

추가적인 정보를 원하시면, 아래에 나온 주소와 전화번호가 적힌 저희 지역 사무소로 **주저하지 마시고 연락 주십시오.**

4 "~을 기대하겠습니다" [맺음말 표현]

▶ 결구에서 '답장을 기다리겠다' 혹은 '곧 뵙게 되길 기대하겠다'라고 할 때 'look forward to + [명사형]'의 관용적 표현이 많이 쓰인다.

> I hope I have covered all the questions you asked. However, do not hesitate to contact me if you need further assistance. **I look forward to** your prompt and positive response to our offer.

귀하께서 하신 모든 질문에 답변이 됐기를 바랍니다. 하지만 도움이 더 필요하시면 바로 연락 주십시오. 저희의 제안에 대해 귀사의 신속하고 긍정적인 답변을 **기대하겠습니다.**

Pattern Practice

1   ~을 담당하고 있습니다.

I am in charge of _____ .

① 연구개발부   the R&D Department
② 신입사원 교육   training new employees
③ 기획팀   the Planning Team

2   ~에 관하여 이메일 드립니다.

I am e-mailing you regarding _____ .

① 저희의 신제품 카탈로그   our new product catalog
② 당신의 제안   your suggestion
③ 초대   the invitation

3   주저하지 마시고 ~에게 연락 주십시오.

Please do not hesitate to contact _____ .

① 736-2031번으로 직접 저에게   me directly at 736-2031
② 질문이 있으시면 즉시 저희에게   us immediately if you have any questions
③ 위에 언급한 번호의 팩스로 저의 비서에게   my secretary by fax at the above-mentioned number

4   ~을 기대하겠습니다.

I look forward to _____ .

① 당신이 조언해 주시길   receiving your advice
② 곧 답변을 듣기를   hearing from you soon
③ 컨퍼런스에서 당신을 만나 뵙기를   meeting you at the conference

Writing Exercise

A Complete the sentences using the given words.

1 제 이름은 김정은이고 마케팅부를 책임지고 있습니다.
(name / in charge of)

▶ _____.

2 저희 회사는 가전제품을 전문으로 다루고 있습니다.
(specialize in / household appliances)

▶ _____.

3 10월 4일에 기록된 귀하의 불만사항 때문에 이메일 드립니다.
(regarding / complaint)

▶ _____.

4 의문점이 있으시면 주저하지 마시고 인사과로 연락 주시기 바랍니다.
(further / hesitate / contact / Personal Department)

▶ _____.

5 저희의 제안에 대한 신속하고 긍정적인 답변을 기대하겠습니다.
(look forward to / response / offer)

▶ _____.

6 만약 이 문제와 관련한 더 많은 정보를 원하시면 언제든 연락 주십시오.
(should / wish to / further / regarding)

▶ _____, please do not hesitate to contact me at the

e-mail address below.

7 저의 노트북 컴퓨터에 있는 몇 가지 문제점 때문에 이메일을 보냅니다.
(regarding / problems / laptop computer)

▶ _____.

8 저희 제품에 대한 자세한 정보를 제공해 드리고자 합니다.
(wish to / provide / detailed information)

▶ _____.

Refer to the Korean and complete the emails.

1 7월 21일에 주신 메일에서 언급하신 문제에 관해 이메일 드립니다. 귀사의 직원들이 언급한 문제와 합병 절차에 관해 좀 더 논의하고 자 5월 5일, 월요일에 시카고에 있는 귀하의 본사를 방문하고자 합니다.

I'm emailing you _____. We would like to visit your head office in Chicago on Monday, May 5, to discuss further the issues your staff raised, and the procedure for the merger.

2 매크로 사의 차장, 마이클 박입니다. 저희 뉴욕 지사 지점장께서 귀하의 성함을 알려 주셨습니다.

I am Assistant Director Michael Park at the Macro Co. _____ the Regional Manager in our New York office.

3 저희 회사의 연료 효율이 좋은 차량들에 관한 자료를 제공해 드리고자 합니다. 이 건과 관련해 추가 자료를 원하시면 주저하지 마시고 736-2307번으로 제게 연락 주십시오.

_____ some of our energy-efficient vehicles. Should you wish to have any further information regarding this matter, please _____ _____ at 736-2307.

+ TRY! 자유롭게 이메일을 써 보세요.

전기그릴 전문 제조회사 N-Grill Company에서 홍보부에서 자사의 최신 전기 그릴(electric grill)을 홍보하고 구입을 장려하는 이메일을 보내 고자 한다. 영국의 신생 패스트푸드 체인점 A&C Food의 홈페이지에서 물품 구매 담당자 Jason Garcia의 이름을 보고, 자사의 신제품 출시를 알리며 귀사와의 거래를 희망한다는 뜻을 비춘다. 또한, 신제품에 관한 추가 정보를 얻을 수 있는 이메일 주소와 회사의 홈페이지 주소도 함께 일 러준다.

■ 정답은 없습니다.

첨부파일 보내기

Subject	New Terms and Conditions
From	leems@han.com
To	stevep@free.com

59.mp3

Dear Mr. Park,

I hope you are well. I am pleased to inform you that we have decided to accept your last offer, so I sent you the contract yesterday by snail mail for security purposes. Please send me an acknowledgement e-mail as soon as you receive it, and send the contract back to us after signing it.

I am also enclosing an attachment of the updated catalog containing all of our brand-new equipment as a PDF file. Please view it with Adobe Reader, and let me know if you experience any difficulties.

Please note that I will be out of the office from October 11 to 12.

Sincerely yours,

Minsu Lee

General Affairs Manager

leems@han.com

제목: 새로운 계약조건

박 선생님께,

잘 지내시는지요. 귀하의 지난 번 제안을 저희가 수락하기로 결정했다는 것을 알려드리게 되어 기쁩니다. 따라서 보안을 위해 어제 우편으로 계약서를 발송했습니다. 받으시는 대로 확인 메일을 보내주시기 바라며, 계약서에 서명하신 후 돌려보내 주시기를 부탁드립니다.

또한, 저희 회사의 새로운 장비들을 모두 포함한 새 카탈로그를 PDF 파일 형태로 첨부하여 보냅니다. Adobe Reader 프로그램을 사용해서 열어보시고, 만약 문제가 있으시면 알려 주십시오.

제가 10월 11일부터 12일까지 사무실을 비우게 되는 점을 유념해 주시기 바랍니다.

친애하는,

이민수

총무부장

leems@han.com

Vocabulary & Expressions

I am pleased to inform you that ... ~을 알려드리게 되어 기쁩니다.

I am pleased to inform you that we have decided to sign the contract.

▶ 저희가 계약을 체결하기로 결정했음을 알려드리게 되어 기쁩니다.

as soon as ~하자마자, ~하는 대로 '가능한 한 빨리'는 as soon as possible

Please hand me the report **as soon as** you finish it.

▶ 보고서 작성을 마치는 대로 제게 제출해 주세요.

for security purposes 보안상의 이유로

For security purposes, may I have your corporate ID number, please?

▶ 보안을 위해서 그러니, 사업자등록번호를 말씀해 주시겠어요?

Please note that ... ~라는 점을 유념해 주세요.

Please note that the our agency will be closed from the 18th until the 22nd.

▶ 저희 영업소는 18일부터 22일까지 문을 닫으니 착오 없으시기 바랍니다.

Let me know 알려 주세요, 연락 주세요

Please **let me know** if you experience any difficulties in viewing the file I sent you.

▶ 제가 보내드린 파일을 보시는 데 어려움이 있으면 알려 주십시오.

Vocabulary Check-Up

Fill in the blanks with the appropriate expressions.

1 확인 이메일을 받았음을 알려드리고자 합니다.

▶ We just want to let you know that we have received your _____ _____.

2 귀하의 지난번 제안을 수락하기로 결정했음을 알려드리게 되어 기쁩니다.

▶ I _____ _____ _____ _____ you that we have decided to accept your last offer.

3 보안상의 이유로, 새 모델의 디자인을 일반 우편으로 부쳤습니다.

▶ I sent you the design of the new model by snail mail _____ _____ _____.

4 계약서에 서명하신 후에 저희에게 돌려보내 주세요.

▶ Please send the contract back to us _____ _____ it.

5 이 HTML 이메일을 보시는 데 어려움이 있으시면 저에게 알려 주세요.

▶ If you _____ _____ _____ viewing this HTML email, please let me know.

1   "~을 첨부합니다." [첨부파일을 보낼 때]

▶ enclose는 '~을 동봉하다'의 의미로, 이메일이 아닌 보통 우편물에서도 사용할 수 있는 단어다. 또한 I am attaching ~을 사용할 수도 있다.

> Thank you for your inquiry. **I am enclosing an attachment** which contains all the information you requested. If you have any questions, please do not hesitate to contact me at lily@ miraesoft.com.

귀하의 문의에 감사드립니다. 요청하신 모든 자료를 포함한 **첨부파일을 함께 보냅니다.** 궁금한 사항이 있으면, 주저하지 마시고 lily@miraesoft.com으로 연락 주십시오.

2   "~을 알리게 되어 기쁩니다." [좋은 소식을 전할 때]

▶ 반대로 그다지 반갑지 않은 소식을 전할 때는 I regret to inform you that ~과 같은 표현을 쓸 수 있다.

> **I am pleased to inform you that** the printed brochures for the 2008 CMA Trade Show have been mailed to you.

2008 CMA 무역박람회에 관한 인쇄된 책자가 우편으로 발송되었다는 것**을 알리게 되어 기쁩니다.**

3   "~으로 파일을 열어보세요." [파일 보는 방법을 알려줄 때]

▶ 파일을 압축하거나 변환해서 보낼 때는 어떤 프로그램을 사용해서 볼 수 있는지에 대한 정보도 함께 알려 주는 것이 좋다. 이때는 view it with ~를 사용하면 된다.

> The contract that I sent you yesterday is in PDF format, so it is not compatible with MS Word. **Please view it with** Adobe Reader. If you do not receive it, please let me know so that I can resend it as soon as possible.

제가 어제 보내드린 계약서는 PDF 형식으로 되어 있어서 MS 워드와는 호환이 안 됩니다. Adobe Reader 프로그램**으로 봐주십시오.** 제대로 받으실 수 없으면 알려 주세요. 최대한 빨리 다시 보내드리겠습니다.

4   "~을 유념해 주십시오." [통지 및 알릴 때]

▶ Please note that ...은 ~한 사실에 유념해 달라는 의미로, 서면상에서 자주 사용하는 표현이다. Make note of ...를 사용할 수도 있다.

> **Please note that** I will be out of the office from October 11, and I shall be back in the office by January 15. Please direct any urgent or outstanding questions to Gary Fitchester at gfitchy@ han.com or call 202-818-2011.

제가 10월 11일에 사무실을 비워서 1월 15일에 돌아옴**을 유념해 주십시오.** 긴급하거나 갑작스런 질문이 생기면 게리 핏체스터 씨에게 gfitchy@han.com이나 202-818-2011로 연락 주시기 바랍니다.

Pattern Practice

1 ~첨부파일을 보냅니다.

I am enclosing an attachment _____.

① 현금 흐름 보고서를 포함한   that has a statement on our cash flow
② 저희 제품의 모든 가격 목록이 담긴   with a price list of the full range of our products
③ 다음 미팅의 일정이 포함된   with the agenda for our next meeting

2 ~을 알리게 되어 기쁩니다.

I am pleased to inform you _____.

① 서류 심사에서 통과하셨다는 것을   that you have passed the documents screening stage
② 그 프로그램은 4월 한 달 동안 공짜라는 것을 that the program is free between April 1 and 30
③ 귀사와 거래하길 원한다는 것을   that we would like to do business with you

3 ~으로 파일을 열어보십시오.

Please view the file with _____.

① OCR 형식으로 돼 있으니 적합한 프로그램으로
an appropriate program since the file is in OCR format

② docx로 저장되어 있으니 Word 2007 프로그램으로
Word 2007 since we have saved it in docx

③ 파일이 압축돼 있으니 Zip 파일 프로그램으로
a Zip file program since the file is compressed

4 ~을 유념해 주세요.

Please note that _____.

① 다음 주 내내 출장 가고 없다는 것을
I will be on a business trip for all of next week

② 오전 10시 이전에는 시간을 낼 수 없다는 것을
I am not available before 10 a.m.

③ 다음 달로 예정되어 있었던 우리 회의가 취소되었음을
our meeting scheduled for next month has been canceled

Writing Exercise

A Complete the sentences using the given words.

1 귀하께서 요청하신 모든 자료가 포함된 첨부파일을 보냅니다.
(enclose / attachment / contain / request)

    ▶ _____.

2 저희의 새로운 카탈로그가 그 상태로 보내기엔 파일 크기가 너무 커서 압축해야 했습니다.
(compress / too ~ to … / as is)

    ▶ _____.

3 파일을 받으시면 그것의 압축을 풀 수 있는 적절한 프로그램을 이용하십시오.
(appropriate / decompress / once / receive)

    ▶ _____.

4 제가 어제 보낸 계약서는 PDF 형식으로 되어 있어서 MS 워드와는 호환이 안 됩니다.
(contract / PDF format / compatible with)

    ▶ _____.

5 같이 보내드리기로 했던 파일을 첨부하지 않고 이메일을 보내서 죄송합니다.
(accept one's apologies / without / be supposed to / enclose)

    ▶ _____.

6 제가 보내드린 파일을 여는 데 문제를 겪으시면 알려 주시기 바랍니다.
(let / if / any problems / open)

    ▶ _____.

7 귀하의 제안을 수락하기로 결정했다는 것을 알려드리게 되어 기쁩니다.
(be pleased to / decide / accept)

    ▶ _____.

8 제가 다음 주 내내 사무실을 비운다는 것을 유념해 주십시오.
(note that … / be out of)

    ▶ _____.

B   Refer to the Korean and complete the emails.

1   요청하신 자료들을 모두 포함한 첨부파일을 보냅니다. 저희의 새로운 카탈로그가 그 상태로 보내기엔 파일 크기가 너무 커서 압축해서 보내야 했습니다. 파일을 받으시면 압축을 풀 수 있는 적절한 프로그램을 이용하십시오.

_____ which contains all the information you requested.

I had to _____ before I sent it to you since the size of file is too big to

send as is. Please _____ once you receive the file.

2   같이 보내드리기로 했던 첨부파일 없이 이메일을 보내드려서 죄송합니다. 첨부해서 다시 이메일 드립니다. 첨부파일은 계약서와 다른 관련 서류들을 포함하고 있습니다. 동봉된 계약서는 PDF 형식으로 되어 있어 MS 워드 프로그램과는 호환되지 않습니다. Adobe Reader 프로그램으로 봐주십시오. 제가 보내드린 파일을 여는 데 문제를 겪으시면 알려 주시기 바랍니다.

Please _____ e-mailing you without the attachment I was supposed to

have enclosed. I am e-mailing you another one with the attachment. The attachment contains the

contract and a few other relevant documents. The enclosed contract is in PDF format, and is not

compatible with MS Word. _____ Adobe Reader. Please _____

_____ opening the file that I sent you.

3   제가 9월 15일에 사무실을 비워서 10월 15일에 돌아옴을 유념해 주십시오. 긴급하거나 갑작스런 질문이 생기면 게리 핏체스터 씨에게 gfitchy@han.com이나 202-818-2011로 연락 주시기 바랍니다. 다른 이메일은 돌아오는 대로 답변 드리겠습니다. 모든 일정은 닉 손튼 씨와 상의하시면 됩니다.

Please _____.
Please direct any urgent or outstanding questions to Gary Fitchester at gfitchy@han.com or call
202-818-2011. I will answer all other e-mails upon my return. All scheduling should go through Nick
Thornton.

+ TRY!   자유롭게 이메일을 써 보세요.

A&C Food의 물품 구매 담당자 Jason Garcia에게 자사에서 그동안 출시한 여러 종류의 전기 그릴을 보여주기 위해, 전자 카탈로그를 파일첨부하여 보내고자 한다.
파일 용량이 꽤 크기 때문에 압축했다는 말과 함께, 파일이 PDF 형식으로 되어 있어서 파일을 열 때는 Adobe Reader 프로그램이 필요하다는 정보도 알려준다. 혹시 파일을 보는 데 문제가 있을 때는 언제든 이메일과 회사 전화로 문의하라고 일러둔다.

■ 정답은 없습니다.

미팅 약속 정하기

Subject	Meeting Schedule
From	janehong@han.com
To	jsmith@free.com

60.mp3

Dear Mr. Smith,

I would like to set up an appointment to see you so that we can discuss the matter further. Please leave a message with my secretary as to when and where we can meet, or alternatively, you could come to my office on Monday at 3 as I will be available after 2 on that day.

I will review the contract before our meeting, and if needed, I will ask for additional information. I will get back to you with the results of the review.

I look forward to meeting you soon.

Sincerely yours,

Jane Hong

General Affairs Manager

janehong@han.com

제목: 회의 일정

스미스 씨께,

약속을 정하여 그 건에 대해 좀 더 논의하고 싶습니다. 만나 뵐 수 있는 시간과 장소를 제 비서에게 남겨 주시거나, 아니면 제가 월요일 2시 이후에 가능하오니 월요일 3시에 저희 사무실로 들러 주시기 바랍니다.

회의 전에 계약서를 검토하고, 필요하다면 추가 정보를 요청하도록 하겠습니다. 검토 결과를 알려드리겠습니다.

그럼 곧 만나 뵙길 기대합니다.

친애하는,

제인 홍

총무부장

janehong@han.com

set up an appointment 약속 날짜를 잡다 set up 대신 make를 쓸 수 있다.

I would like to **set up an appointment** to see you so that we can further discuss the matter.

▶ 약속 날짜를 잡아서 만나 뵙고 그 문제에 관해 자세히 논의했으면 합니다.

Please leave a message with ~에게 메시지를 남겨 주세요.

Please leave a message with my secretary when I'm not in the office.

▶ 제가 사무실에 없을 때는 제 비서에게 메시지를 남겨 주세요.

alternatively 다른 안으로는, 양자택일로 어떤 안을 내놓은 후, 그것이 가능하지 않을 경우의 대안을 제시하며 문두에 사용하는 표현

Alternatively, you can come to my office at 4 p.m.

▶ 아니면, 오후 4시에 저희 사무실로 와 주셔도 됩니다.

back to ~에게 연락하다, 답장을 주다 전화 또는 이메일 등으로 연락을 다시 주겠다고 할 때에 get back to를 사용한다.

I'll **get back to** you as soon as possible.

▶ 가능한 한 빨리 연락 드릴게요.

be available 시간이 있는 시간을 낼 수 없는 상황이어서 약속을 잡을 수 없을 때는 have no time보다 세련된 표현으로 not available을 쓸 수 있다.

I am afraid I will not **be available** to see you for the next two weeks.

▶ 유감스럽게도 앞으로 2주 동안은 시간이 없어 만날 수가 없겠네요.

Fill in the blanks with the appropriate expressions.

1 저희 사무실로 오시거나, 아니면 다른 방법으로 귀사 근처에서 뵐 수도 있어요.

▶ You could come to my office, or _____, I could meet you near your company.

2 다음 회의를 위한 일정을 잡고 싶습니다.

▶ I'd like to _____ _____ _____ _____ for our next meeting.

3 죄송하지만 다음 주 금요일에는 만날 수가 없겠네요.

▶ I am afraid I will _____ _____ _____ to see you next Friday.

4 컨퍼런스 날짜에 대한 메시지를 제 동료에게 남겨주세요.

▶ Please _____ _____ _____ _____ my co-worker about the date of the conference.

5 이메일 받으시면 답장 주세요.

▶ Please _____ _____ _____ me when you receive my e-mail.

1 "직접 만나 뵙고 싶습니다" [미팅 약속을 잡을 때]

▶ 미팅 일정을 잡을 때는 if possible을 넣어 좀 더 공손하게 말할 수 있다. discuss 다음에는 전치사 없이 목적어가 바로 오는 것에 주의하자.

> **I'd like to see you in person, if possible, to discuss** further our next year's project rather than talking to you over the phone or by e-mail. As you know, we need to come to consensus very soon, and it is more likely that we can come to some sort of decision if we meet in person.

가능하시다면, 전화나 이메일로 얘기 나누는 것보다 **직접 만나 뵙고** 다음 해 프로젝트에 관해 좀 더 논의 드리고 싶습니다. 아시다시피, 빨리 의견 일치를 봐야 하는데요, 직접 만난다면 쉽게 어떤 결정에 도달할 수 있을 것 같습니다.

2 "~(날짜)가 저도 좋습니다." [약속 날짜 시간을 수락할 때]

▶ would be okay for[with] me에서 okay 대신 fine을 쓸 수도 있다.

> Thank you for giving the opportunity to see you. 3 o'clock on November 5 **would be okay for me** to meet you as well. Please let me know if you have a place in mind, as I have no preference at this point. I await your reply.

만날 기회를 주셔서 감사합니다. 11월 5일 3시에 만나는 것**이 저도 좋습니다.** 지금 원하는 곳이 따로 없으니 염두에 두신 장소가 있으시면 알려 주십시오. 답변을 기다리겠습니다.

3 "~에서 만나는 게 좋겠습니다." [약속 장소를 정할 때]

▶ It would help me greatly if …는 직역하면 '~할 수 있다면 저에겐 매우 도움이 되겠습니다'의 의미로, 매우 격식을 차린 공손한 표현이다.

> **It would help me greatly if we met** at the Grand Hotel on Wednesday the 13th. I have a few meetings that I have to attend until 4 p.m. that day, and the last meeting is nearby. I can meet you in 4:30 at the Grand Hotel, so long as you are okay with coming to the hotel.

13일 수요일에 그랜드 호텔**에서 만나 뵈면 좋겠습니다.** 그날 4시까지 참석해야 할 회의가 몇 개 있고 근처에서 마지막 회의가 있습니다. 오시는 게 괜찮으시면 그랜드 호텔에서 4시 30분에 만날 수 있습니다.

4 "다른 날로 변경해야겠습니다." [약속을 변경할 때]

▶ 회의 일정 등을 변경할 때는 change the meeting이 아니라 reschedule the meeting이라고 해야 한다는 것에 주의하자.

> I know I was supposed to meet you at 2, but something came up, so **I need to reschedule our meeting** for another day. I will be free next Monday and Thursday after 2 p.m. I hope you are free around one of those times so I can finally meet you.

2시에 만나 뵙기로 했었지만 일이 생겨서 **회의를 다른 날로 다시 잡아야겠습니다.** 다음 주 월요일과 화요일 2시 이후에 시간이 납니다. 그때쯤 시간이 나시면 만나뵙길 바라겠습니다.

Pattern Practice

1 가능하다면 직접 뵙고 ~에 관해 논의하고 싶습니다.

I'd like to see you in person, if possible, to discuss _____ .

① 새로운 고용 기준   the new criteria for hiring
② 당신의 새로운 책무   your new responsibilities
③ 임원들을 위한 축하연 준비   the arrangements for the board members banquet

2 ~가 …하기에 저한테 좋겠습니다.

_____ **would be okay for me** _____ .

① 오늘 오후가, 당신을 만나기에   This afternoon / to meet you
② 금요일 오전이, 당신의 사무실에 들르기에   Friday morning / to drop by your office
③ 8월 5일이, 출장을 가기에   August 5 / to go on a business trip

3 ~에서 만나면 좋겠습니다

It would help me greatly if we met _____ .

① 3월 2일에 대회의장에서   at the conference center on March 2
② 3시에 본사에서   at the head office at 3 p.m.
③ 가급적 12월 첫째 주에 보스턴에서   in Boston, preferably during the first week of December

4 ~일정을 변경해야겠습니다.

I need to reschedule _____ .

① 악천후로 인해 회의를 다음달로   the meeting for next month due to the bad weather
② 약속을 몇 시간 후로   the appointment to some time later
③ 화상 회의를 다른 날로   the video conference for another day

Writing Exercise

A Complete the sentences using the given words.

1 가능하다면 직접 만나서 다음 연도의 프로젝트에 관해 얘기하고 싶습니다.
(in person / discuss / if possible)

▶ _____ .

2 저는 다음 주 금요일 오후 12시에 시간이 됩니다.
(be free / next)

▶ _____ .

3 11월 5일 3시가 만나기에 좋겠습니다.
(be okay / for me)

▶ _____ .

4 수요일에 그랜드 호텔에서 만나는 게 좋겠습니다.
(It would help me greatly / if)

▶ _____ .

5 회의를 다른 날로 변경해야겠습니다.
(need / reschedule / another day)

▶ _____ .

6 저는 수요일에 대략 오전 11시부터 오후 1시 사이에 시간이 납니다.
(be available / from ... to / approximately)

▶ _____ .

7 월요일 오전 10시에 뵙기로 했었는데 일이 좀 생겼습니다.
(know / be supposed to / come up)

▶ _____ .

8 혹시 생각해 두신 장소가 있다면 말씀해 주십시오.
(let someone know / if / have ... in mind)

▶ _____ .

B Refer to the Korean and complete the emails.

1 가능하다면, 직접 만나 뵙고 새로운 프로젝트에 관해 귀하의 의견을 들었으면 합니다. 화요일 3시가 어떠신가요? 편하신 시간을 알려 주세요. 그때 뵈러 가겠습니다.

> _____, I'd like to see you in person and hear your opinion on this new project. _____? _____ when is convenient for you. I can come see you at that time.

2 내일 귀하의 사무실을 찾아뵈려고 했지만, 유감스럽게도 약속을 못 지킬 것 같습니다. 그래서 회의를 다른 날짜로 변경해야겠습니다. 다음 주 목요일 2시가 어떠십니까? 약속 변경 요청으로 불편을 끼쳐드려 대단히 죄송합니다.

> I was going to visit your office tomorrow, but I'm afraid I cannot make it. So I _____ _____. How about the following Thursday at 2:00? I am _____ in asking you to make this change.

3 계약서를 검토하면서 필요하면 추가 자료를 요청하겠습니다. 화요일까지 검토 결과를 가지고 연락 드리겠습니다.

> I will review the contract, and if needed, I will _____. I will _____ with the result of the review.

+ TRY! 자유롭게 이메일을 써 보세요.

> A&C Food 사의 Jason Garcia로부터 직접 만나서 물품거래 계약사항에 대해 자세히 논의하자는 제안 메일을 받고 답장을 쓰려고 한다. Sarah는 이번 주 수요일부터 금요일까지 시간이 나는데, BNC Hotel 식당에서 보는 게 어떤지 묻는다. 아니면, 수요일 또는 목요일 오후 3시에 직접 A&C Food 사를 방문할 수도 있다고 얘기한다. 다음 주부터는 2주간 휴가를 가기 때문에 가급적 이번 주에 미팅이 이뤄졌으면 좋겠다는 뜻도 비친다.

■ 정답은 없습니다.

동료 간의 인사 메일

A Social E-mail Between Colleagues

Subject	Thank you.
From	brucelee@han.com
To	all@free.com

61.mp3

To everyone,

I would like to thank all of you for attending my retirement party yesterday. I was extremely impressed with your warm-hearted farewell.

I took the position of CEO exactly 10 years ago. I really appreciate that I had the support of each and every one of you. Without you, I wouldn't have enjoyed working here.

Thank you again for your hard work, support, and friendship.

I will remember all of you forever.

Sincerely yours,

Bruce Lee

CEO

brucelee@han.com

제목: 감사합니다.
친애하는 직원 여러분,
어제 저의 은퇴 기념식에 참석해 주신 모든 분께 감사의 말씀을 드립니다. 저는 여러분들의 따뜻한 고별식에 깊이 감동 받았습니다.
저는 정확히 10년 전에 CEO 자리에 취임했습니다. 여러분 개개인이 저에게 주신 후원에 진심으로 감사드립니다. 여러분이 없었다면, 전 즐겁게 일할 수 없었을 것입니다.
여러분의 수고와 지지, 그리고 우정에 다시 한번 감사드립니다.
여러분 모두를 영원히 기억할 것입니다.
친애하는,
브루스 리
CEO
bruecelee@han.com

Vocabulary & Expressions

I would like to thank A for B B에 대해 A에게 감사드립니다 전치사 for 다음에 감사하는 이유가 명사 형태로 온다.

I would like to thank him **for** his support while writing this book.
▶ 저는 이 책을 쓰는 동안 그의 지원에 감사드립니다.

I was extremely impressed with[by] ~에 대해 크게 감동받았습니다

I was extremely impressed with his thoughtful e-mail.
▶ 저는 그의 사려 깊은 이메일에 크게 감동 받았습니다.

take the position of ~의 직책을 맡다

Mr. Lee **took the position of** Executive Director at the company after 15 years of hard work.
▶ 이 선생님은 15년간의 수고 끝에 회사의 전무이사직을 맡게 되었다.

I really appreciate that ~ ~에 대해 깊이 감사드립니다 Thank you for ~보다 격식 차린 표현

I really appreciate that you are taking care of everything.
▶ 여러모로 신경 써 주셔서 감사합니다.

Without you 만약 당신이(당신의 도움이) 없었다면 If I had been without you의 의미로 가정의 뜻을 나타내고 있다.

Without you, I would not have been able to have become a good salesman.
▶ 당신의 도움이 없었다면 저는 훌륭한 영업사원이 될 수 없었을 거예요.

Vocabulary Check-Up

Fill in the blanks with the appropriate expressions.

1 당신의 정직성에 깊이 감동 받았습니다.

▶ I _____ really _____ _____ your honesty.

2 이 문제의 해결 방법에 대해 제게 해준 모든 충고에 정말 감사드립니다.

▶ I really _____ all the advice you gave me on _____ _____ solve these problems.

3 은퇴 파티를 마련해 주시다니 정말 사려 깊으시군요.

▶ It was very _____ _____ you to have a retirement party for me.

4 열심히 일해 주신 것에 다시 한번 감사드립니다.

▶ _____ _____ _____ for your hard work.

5 당신이 없었다면, 우리는 개선 작업에 성공하지 못했을 거예요.

▶ Without you, we _____ not _____ _____ in implementing the changes.

6 마이클은 작년에 영업부장의 직책을 맡았습니다.

▶ Michael _____ _____ _____ of Manager in the Sales Department last year.

Actual Sample

1 "승진을 축하드립니다." [축하 인사할 때]

▶ '~을 축하한다'고 말할 때 전치사 on 다음에 축하의 이유가 온다. Congratulations에서 마지막 -s도 빼먹지 않도록 주의하자.

> **Congratulations on** your promotion! There isn't a better person for that important job. And thank you for everything that you did for me while I was staying in London. If you visit Korea in the future, please let me know.

승진을 **축하드립니다**! 그런 요직에 (당신보다) 더 나은 적임자는 없습니다. 런던에 있는 동안 저를 위해 해주신 모든 것에 감사드립니다. 나중에 한국에 오시게 되면, 알려 주세요.

2 "서울로 전근하게 되었습니다." [전근 인사할 때]

▶ 미래 진행형을 사용해 I will be transferring to ...라고 해도 된다. 승진했을 때는 be promoted to [직책], 퇴사 시에는 quit 또는 resign을 이용한다.

> As a result of the October 10 personnel changes, **I will be transferred to** the Seoul office. I will start working there from November. Thank you for everything you have done for me during my tenure with this branch.

10월 10일에 인사 변동의 결과로, 서울 사무소**로 전근하게 되었습니다**. 그곳에서 11월부터 일할 것입니다. 이곳의 지사에서 근무하는 동안 저를 위해 해주신 모든 것들에 감사드립니다.

3 "늦어진 점에 대해 사과드립니다." [사과할 때]

▶ would like to apologize for ...를 사용해 좀 더 정중하게 말할 수도 있다. 사과를 받아 달라고 할 때는 Please accept my apologies for ....

> **I apologize for** the delay. I was working on something else and thought your project could wait. I am sorry that you were inconvenienced. What should I do first to solve this problem? Let me know what you think.

늦어진 점**에 대해 사과드립니다**. 다른 일을 진행하는 중이었고 귀하의 프로젝트는 여유가 있을 거라고 생각했습니다. 불편을 끼쳐 죄송합니다. 문제를 해결하려면 제가 무엇부터 해야 할까요? 이에 대해 어떻게 생각하시는지 알려 주십시오.

4 "힘든 시기를 겪고 계시다고 들었습니다." [격려 및 위로할 때]

▶ I heard that 뒤에는 '주어+동사'의 형태로 전해 들은 소식이 온다. I heard about ...이라고 말할 때는 뒤에 명사 또는 명사형이 온다.

> **I heard that** JJ is going to close its Seoul branch. I wanted to let you know that our thoughts and prayers are with you all during this most difficult time. I'm sure that everything will work itself out if you give it time.

JJ가 서울 지사 근처로 갈 거란 **소식을 들었습니다**. 이토록 힘든 시기를 겪고 계시지만 저희의 걱정과 기도가 함께한다는 것을 알아주십시오. 시간을 두고 보시면, 모든 일이 잘 풀릴 거라 확신합니다.

Pattern Practice

1 ~을 축하드립니다

Congratulations on _____!

① 새로운 프로젝트의 성공   your success with the new project

② 새로운 직장을 구한 것   your new job

③ 새로운 가게의 개업   the opening of your new store

2 제가 ~로 전근하게 됐습니다.

I will be transferred _____.

① 다시 스테이플스 센터로   back over to the Staples Center

② 곧 뉴욕지사로   to the New York branch soon

③ 4월부터 다른 회사로   to another company from April

3 ~에 대해서 사과드립니다.

I apologize for _____.

① 혼동   the mix-up

② 아침 회의가 연기된 것   postponing this morning's conference

③ 잘못된 정보를 보낸 것   sending you the wrong information

4 ~라고 들었습니다.

I heard that _____.

① 당신이 곤경에 처해 있다고

   you are having some problems

② 당신의 프로젝트가 취소되었다고

   your project has been canceled

③ 당신의 회사가 LA 지사 근처로 갈 예정이라고

   your company is going to close its LA branch

Writing Exercise

A   Complete the sentences using the given words.

1   바쁘신 데도 저희와 함께 자리해 주셔서 감사합니다.
(thanks for / be with)

▶ _____ .

2   저는 대전 지사로 전근 가게 됐습니다.
(be transferred to)

▶ _____ .

3   매우 힘든 일을 겪고 계시다고 들었습니다.
(heard / some problems)

▶ _____ .

4   이런 말씀드리기 죄송하지만 저는 그 파티에 갈 수 없습니다.
(be sorry to say / come to)

▶ _____ .

5   시간 나는 대로 전화 주시면 고맙겠습니다.
(appreciate / if / as soon as / get a chance)

▶ _____ .

6   이번에 과장으로 승진하셨다고 들었습니다.
(hear / be promoted to / section chief)

▶ _____ .

7   저희 팀을 대표하여, 당신의 퇴임에 축복을 기원합니다.
(on behalf of / wish / good luck)

▶ _____ .

8   인천 사무소에 저희 기술 엔지니어들을 신속히 보내 드리지 못한 점에 대해 사과드리고 싶습니다.
(would like to apologize for / delay / engineers)

▶ _____ .

Refer to the Korean and complete the emails.

1 지금까지 오랫동안 거래를 해오고 있지만, 귀사는 언제나 결제일을 지켜오셨습니다. 귀사가 없었더라면, 저희 회사는 큰 곤경에 처했을 것입니다. 귀사와 함께 일하게 되어 매우 기쁘며, 도움에 대해 다시 한번 감사드립니다.

> We have been doing business for a long time now, and you have always paid your bills by the due date. _____, _____. I am very pleased to work with you. _____.

2 포항 사무소로 전근 가게 되었습니다. 제 후임자는 강철 씨입니다. 그는 대구 지사장에서 이사로 근무하다 방금 돌아왔습니다. 저의 새 연락처는 나중에 알려드리겠습니다. 당분간은 제 개인 이메일로 연락 주시기 바랍니다.

> _____ our Pohang Office. _____ Mr. Kang Chul. He has just returned from his position as Managing Director of the Daegu Branch. _____. But in the meantime I can be contacted via e-mail at my personal email address.

3 오늘 주문하신 물품을 배송했습니다. 배송이 늦어진 점에 대해 사과드립니다. 사과의 뜻으로 할인쿠폰을 첨부하였습니다. 이 쿠폰이 있으면 다음 구매 시에 50% 할인해 드립니다. 마음에 드셨으면 좋겠습니다.

> We sent your order today. _____. We have included a discount coupon as our way of apologizing. This coupon entitles you to 50% off your next purchase. _____.

+ TRY! 자유롭게 이메일을 써 보세요.

> A&C Food 사의 Jason Garcia가 자재관리 전무이사(Executive Director)로 승진했다는 소식을 듣고 축하 이메일을 보내려고 한다. 그러한 요직에 적임자라는 칭송과 더불어, 그동안 자사와의 거래에 힘써 준 것에 감사를 표한다. 축하의 뜻으로 화분을 오늘 보냈으니 내일 오후쯤 도착한다는 것도 알린다.

■ 정답은 없습니다.

Peter F. Drucker
"The Father of Modern Management"

Peter F. Drucker, the son of a high-level civil servant in the Habsburg Empire and who became a writer, management consultant, and university professor, was born in a suburb of Vienna on November 19, 1909. In his life, he made famous the term "knowledge worker".

Drucker went to Germany and worked as a clerk-trainee for an export firm while [1]**enrolled in** Hamburg University Law School. However, he failed to attend classes as the school did not offer night classes. Then, he traveled to Frankfurt, worked as a financial writer, and finally earned a doctorate in public law and international relations from the University of Frankfurt in 1931 without ever attending class. In 1933, Drucker left Germany for London to escape the Nazis and worked as a securities analyst for an insurance company and then as an economist at a small bank. During that period, his focus [2]**shifted from** economics to people.

In 1943, General Motors asked Drucker to study its management practices, and he [3]**accepted** the job despite his friends' better judgment of the possibility of it destroying his academic reputation. He spent 18 months researching and wrote *Concept of the Corporation*. Yet it was not GM who [4]**favored** his theories but Henry Ford II of the Ford Motor Company. Ford used Drucker's ideas to restructure his company. He [5]**was awarded** the Presidential Medal of Freedom by President George W. Bush on July 9, 2002, and was the Honorary Chairman of the Peter F. Drucker Foundation for Nonprofit Management.

피터 F. 드러커 — "현대 경영학의 아버지"
작가이자 경영 컨설턴트, 대학 교수였던 피터 F. 드러커는 1909년 11월 19일, 비엔나의 어느 교외에서 합스부르크 제국의 고위 공무원의 아들로 태어났다. 그는 성인이 되어 '지식근로자'라는 용어를 유명하게 만들었다. 드러커는 독일로 가서 함부르크 대학 법학부에서 수학하는 동안 한 수출업체의 견습사원으로 일했다. 하지만 학교가 야간 수업을 제공하지 않아 수업엔 참석하지 못했다. 그 후 그는 프랑크푸르트를 여행하며 재정 서기로 일하다가, 1931년에 마침내 출석 한 번 안 하고 프랑크푸르트 대학으로부터 공법과 국제법 전공으로 박사 학위를 받는다. 1933년, 드러커는 나치를 피해 독일에서 런던으로 이주하여 한 보험사에서 증권분석가로 일했고, 후에는 작은 은행에서 경제학자로 근무하였다. 그러는 동안 그의 관심은 경제학에서 사람으로 옮겨갔다. 1943년엔 제너럴 모터스 사에서 드러커에게 회사의 경영방법을 연구해달라고 부탁하였고, 자신의 학문적 명성을 해칠 수도 있다는 친구의 판단에도 불구하고 요청을 수락한다. 그는 18개월 동안의 조사 후에, 〈기업의 개념〉을 집필하였다. 하지만 제너럴 모터스 사는 그의 이론을 지지하지 않았고 포드 모터 사의 헨리 포드 2세가 호의를 보였다. 포드는 회사를 구조조정하는 데 드러커의 아이디어들을 활용하였다. 드러커는 2002년 7월 9일에 조지 부시 대통령으로부터 대통령 자유 훈장을 수여받았으며, 비영리 경영을 위한 Peter F. Drucker 재단의 명예회장을 지냈다.

www.leadertoleader.org

1 be enrolled in (학원·학교 등)에 수업 등록하다

I'm enrolled in the computer engineering program at college.
나는 대학의 전산학 프로그램에 등록했다.

2 shift from A to B A에서 B로 옮기다, 이동하다

Media attention has **shifted** recently **from** political **to** environmental issues.
언론 매체의 관심은 최근 정치문제에서 환경문제로 옮겨가고 있다.

3 accept 수락하다

I am happy to **accept** your invitation.
당신의 초대를 기꺼이 수락하겠습니다.

4 favor 호의를 보이다, 찬성하다

▶ 어떤 것을 더 좋아하여 호의를 보이는 것을 favor라고 하는데, 제안이나 정책에 찬성할 때에도 사용할 수 있다.

In the survey, a majority of people **favored** higher taxes and better public services rather than tax cuts.
설문조사에 의하면, 대다수 사람들은 세금 감면보다 오히려 높은 세금과 더 나은 공공서비스를 선호했다.

5 be awarded ~을 받다(= be granted)

▶ award는 '수여하다'라는 의미의 타동사로도 쓰인다.

Marcy **was awarded** first prize in the essay competition.
마시는 수필 대회에서 1등 상을 받았다.

Who is Peter F. Drucker?

피터 F. 드러커는 '지식 근로자'와 '목표관리'라는 용어를 만들어낸 선구적인 경영 이론가로, 스스로를 '사회생태학자(social ecologist)'라고 불렀다. 비즈니스 경영의 권위자인 드러커는 Leader to Leader 재단을 설립했으며, 30권이 넘는 경영에 관련 서적을 저술하였는데, 인간, 사업, 정부기관, 비영리단체가 어떻게 조직화되는가에 대해 탐구하는 내용으로, 그의 저서는 학문적으로나 대중적으로 널리 읽혔다. 20세기 후반의 많은 변화를 예측하여 명성을 얻었으며, 2002년에는 조지 부시 대통령으로부터 대통령 자유 훈장을 받았다.

Peter F. Drucker Says...

"Management by objectives works if you first think through your objectives. Ninety percent of the time you haven't."

목표관리는 먼저 당신의 목표를 충분히 생각해야만 작용합니다. 우리는 목표를 염두에 두지 않고 90%의 시간을 보냅니다.

"The aim of marketing is to know and understand the customer so well that the product or service fits him and sells itself."

마케팅의 목표는 소비자가 어떤 제품과 서비스를 원하고 무엇을 사는지에 대한 것만큼, 고객에 대해 잘 알고 이해하는 것입니다.

"The most important thing in communication is to hear what isn't being said."

커뮤니케이션에서 가장 중요한 것은 말하지 않은 걸 듣는 것입니다.

Answers & Audio Scripts

WEEK 01 \ 전화 걸고 받기

Vocabulary Check-up p.13

A 1 ⓐ 2 ⓒ 3 ⓔ 4 ⓑ 5 ⓓ

B 1 pick up
2 speak to
3 smartphone
4 in charge of

C 1 This is
2 extension
3 calling
4 Hold
5 put / through

Conversation 1 전화 걸고 받기 p.14   01.mp3

A: 안녕하세요. DRK 사의 사라 테일러입니다. 무엇을 도와 드릴까요?

B: 네, 안녕하세요, 테일러 씨. 마케팅 부서의 스미스 씨와 통화할 수 있을까요?

A: 전화 거신 분이 누구신지 여쭤봐도 될까요?

B: KTS사의 이민수입니다.

A: 네, 지금 전화를 돌려 드리겠습니다. 잠시만 기다리세요.

B: 네, 기다리겠습니다. 감사합니다

Conversation 2 전화 바꿔주기 p.15   02.mp3

A: HM 서비스의 레이첼입니다. 무엇을 도와 드릴까요?

B: 로버트 디거 씨와 통화하고 싶은데요.

A: 잠시만요. 연결해 드리겠습니다.

B: (잠시 후에) 여보세요? 로버트 씨가 금방 나가신 것 같습니다.

A: 음, 그러면 잠시 후에 다시 걸겠습니다. 그분의 내선 번호 좀 알려 주시겠습니까?

B: 그럼요, 322번입니다.

A: 고맙습니다.

Practice 1 Let's Speak p.16

A 1 How / May
2 afraid / back
3 transfer / on
4 reach / extension

B 1 May I ask who's calling, please?
2 I'll put you through now.
3 I'm afraid he's in a meeting now.
4 Who are you trying to reach?

Practice 2 Listen-up p.17

Audio Script – A   03.mp3

A   Good morning. ABC Associates.

B   Hello, may I speak to Mr. Park, please?

A   Please hold while I put you through.

B   Thanks.

C   Hello, this is Jason Park. Who's calling?

B   This is John Kim of the AD Company. I'm calling to remind you of your appointment with Mr. Brown tomorrow.

A   안녕하세요. ABC 조합입니다.

B   여보세요, 미스터 박과 통화할 수 있을까요?

A   전화를 연결하는 동안 기다려 주세요.

B   고맙습니다.

C   여보세요, 제이슨 박입니다. 누구신가요?

B   AD 사의 존 킴입니다. 내일 브라운 씨와의 약속을 상기시켜 드리려고 전화했어요.

Audio Script – B, C   04.mp3

Helen   Good morning, Axa Electronics, Helen Watson speaking. How may I help you?

Sungmin   I'd like to speak to Mr. White, please. I don't have his extension though.

Helen   May I ask who is calling?

Sungmin   Oh, sorry. This is Kim Sungmin from M.I. International.

Helen   Just a moment, please. I will see if he's in.

Sungmin   Sure. I'll hold.

Helen   I am sorry, Mr. Kim. But he's not available at the moment. Would you like to leave a message?

Sungmin   That's okay. I will try to call him another time. Thank you.

Helen   Good day, sir.

헬렌   안녕하세요, Axa 전자의 헬렌 왓슨입니다. 무엇을 도와 드릴까요?

성민   화이트 씨와 통화하고 싶습니다. 내선번호를 몰라서요.

헬렌   실례지만 전화 거신 분은 누구신가요?

성민   아, 죄송합니다. M.I. 인터네셔널의 김성민입니다.

헬렌   잠시만 기다려 주십시오. 안에 계신지 확인해 보겠습니다.

성민   네, 기다릴게요.

헬렌   김선생님, 죄송하지만 그분은 지금 통화하실 수 없습니다. 메시지를 남기시겠어요?

성민   괜찮습니다. 다음에 다시 전화하죠. 감사합니다.

헬렌   좋은 하루 보내세요.

A 1 T 2 F 3 F

B 1 The caller is Kim Sungmin.
2 The caller wants to speak to Mr. White.
3 No, he does not.
4 No, he doesn't because he will call him another time.

C 1 Good morning
2 don't have his extension
3 ask who is calling
4 will see if he's in
5 not available at the moment
6 try to call him another time

WEEK 02 \ 메시지 남기고 받기

Vocabulary Check-up p.19

A 1 ⓑ 2 ⓐ 3 ⓓ 4 ⓔ 5 ⓒ

B 1 ask her to call
2 leave a message
3 as soon as
4 have / name / contact number

C 1 spell 2 called
3 repeat
4 business trip
5 read / back

Conversation 1 메시지 남기기 p.20   07.mp3

A: 여보세요. 저는 데이턴 리서치의 미셸 애스턴입니다. 테리 블랙 씨와 통화할 수 있을까요?
B: 죄송하지만 출장 중이십니다.
A: 언제 돌아오는지 아시나요?
B: 월요일에 돌아옵니다. 메시지를 받아둘까요?
A: 네. 저희 일정에 변동이 생겨서요. 돌아오자마자 저에게 전화해 달라고 해주시겠습니까?
B: 알겠습니다. 블랙 씨가 돌아오면 전달해 드리겠습니다.
A: 감사합니다.

Conversation 2 메시지 받기 p.21   06.mp3

A: 메시지를 남기시겠습니까?
B: 최대한 빨리 저에게 전화해 달라고 해주시겠어요?
A: 알겠습니다. 성함과 연락처를 알려 주시겠어요?
B: 물론이죠. 저는 닉 앤더슨이고 연락처는 07890-255-401입니다.
A: 성함의 철자를 불러주시겠어요?
B: 네. N-I-C-K, A-N-D-E-R-S-O-N입니다. November 할 때 N, India 할 때 I, Charlie 할 때 C, Korea 할 때 K입니다.
A: 다시 확인해 보겠습니다. November의 N, India의 I, Charlie의 C, Korea의 K…
B: 맞습니다.

Practice 1 Let's Speak p.22

A 1 leave / call 2 stepped out / try / later
3 When / back 4 get / pass

B 1 Could I take a message? / Please tell him to call me as soon as he comes back.
2 May I have your name and contact number, please?
3 He will be back in an hour.
4 He is on another line now.

Practice 2 Listen-up p.23

Audio Script – A, B   07.mp3

Receiver	Good morning. National Trading Company.
Caller	Hello. I'd like to speak to Barbara White.
Receiver	I'm sorry she's in a meeting right now. Would you like to leave a message?
Caller	Yes. My name is Emma Elite. Please ask Ms. White to call me on my cell phone.
Receiver	Could you spell your name, please?
Caller	That's E-M-M-A, E-L-I-T-E.
Receiver	Okay, does she have your cell phone number?
Caller	Oh, it's 013-465-8809.
Receiver	All right. Let me read that back. It's zero one three, four six five, double eight nine oh.
Caller	Actually, that should be double eight oh nine.
Receiver	I'm sorry about that. All right. I'll pass on your message.
Caller	Thank you very much. Goodbye.

받은 사람	안녕하세요. 내셔널 무역회사입니다.
건 사람	안녕하세요. 바바라 화이트 씨와 통화하고 싶은데요.
받은 사람	죄송하지만 지금 회의 중이십니다. 용건을 남기시겠어요?
건 사람	네. 제 이름은 엠마 엘리트입니다. 화이트 씨께 제 휴대전화로 전화해 달라고 전해주세요.
받은 사람	성함의 철자를 불러주시겠어요?
건 사람	E-M-M-A, E-L-I-T-E입니다.
받은 사람	알겠습니다. 화이트 씨께서 선생님의 휴대전화 번호를 아시나요?
건 사람	아, 013-465-8809입니다.
받은 사람	네. 확인차 읽어볼게요. 013-465-8890.
건 사람	8809가 되어야 해요.
받은 사람	죄송합니다. 자, 됐습니다. 메시지를 전해 드리겠습니다.
건 사람	감사합니다. 안녕히 계세요.

A 1 The caller's name is Emma Elite.
2 Ms. White is in a meeting.
3 013-465-8809

B 1 I'd like to speak
2 to leave a message
3 call me on my cell phone
4 spell your name
5 read that back
6 double eight nine oh
7 pass on your message

Vocabulary Check-up p.25

A 1 ⓑ 2 ⓔ 3 ⓒ 4 ⓐ 5 ⓓ

B 1 have dialed
   2 wrong extension
   3 Isn't this
   4 There is

C 1 reached
   2 What number
   3 the wrong number
   4 with[by] that name
   5 get back

Conversation 1 잘못 걸린 전화 받기 p.26   08.mp3

A: 여보세요? 클라크 씨와 통화할 수 있을까요?
B: 죄송하지만 몇 번으로 전화하셨나요?
A: 729-4013번 아닌가요?
B: 찾는 분이 누구시죠?
A: 제인 클라크라는 사람을 찾습니다.
B: 전화를 잘못 거신 것 같네요. 그런 이름 가진 분은 여기 없습니다.
A: 미안합니다.
B: 괜찮습니다.

Conversation 2 자동응답기에 메시지 남기기 p.27   09.mp3

A: 리사의 전화입니다. 죄송하지만 지금은 제가 전화를 받을 수 없습니다. 용
   건을 남겨주시면 가능한 한 빨리 연락 드리겠습니다. 삐 소리 후 메시지를
   남겨주세요.
C: 안녕하세요, 리차드슨 씨. 로렌스 밀러입니다. 이번 달에 있을 월례회의의
   일정이 바뀌어 전화 드렸습니다. 가능한 한 빨리 이에 관해 얘기를 나눠야
   하니, 시간 되실 때 연락 주시기 바랍니다.

Practice 1 Let's Speak p.28

A 1 ⓑ 2 ⓒ 3 ⓐ 4 ⓓ 5 ⓔ

B 1 What number did you dial[call]? / Isn't this 555-2357? /
     There's nobody with that name here.
   2 I'm calling regarding our appointment time / call me
     when you get a chance

Practice 2 Listen-up p.29

Audio Script – A, B   10.mp3

Answering machine

You are trying to reach Paul's phone. I am sorry I'm
not available at the moment, but if you leave a
message, I'll get back to you as soon as I can. Please
leave a message after the beep.

Voice message

Hi, Mr. Miller. This is Nancy, Nancy Richardson. I am
returning your call regarding the change of schedule
for our meeting. I guess you are not there to take my
call. I will try to call again later today.

Answering machine

To listen to your message, press 1. If you wish to
change your message, press 2. If you wish to delete
your message, press 3. Alternatively, press the pound
key (#) if you wish to save your message.

자동응답기 폴의 전화입니다. 죄송하지만 지금 제가 전화를 받을 수 없으므로, 메시
지를 남겨주시면 가능한 한 빨리 전화 드리겠습니다. 삐 소리가 난 후 메
세지를 남겨주십시오.

음성 메시지 안녕하세요, 밀러 씨. 낸시 리차드슨입니다. 이번 미팅 일정 변동과 관련
한 전화를 받고 연락 드립니다. 지금 부재중이어서 전화를 받으실 수 없
는 것 같으니, 오늘 중으로 다시 전화하겠습니다.

자동응답기 메시지를 듣고 싶으시면, 1번을 눌러주십시오. 메시지를 바꾸려면 2번
을, 삭제하시려면 3번을 누르십시오. 메시지를 저장하시려면 #버튼을 눌
러주십시오.

A 1 F 2 F 3 T

B 1 This is
   2 returning your call regarding
   3 to take my call
   4 to call again
   5 listen to
   6 change
   7 delete
   8 pound key
   9 save

PLUS WEEK \ 통화 중 문제 발생과 국제전화

Vocabulary Check-up p.31

A 1 ⓓ 2 ⓐ 3 ⓑ 4 ⓒ 5 ⓔ

B 1 breaking up
   2 busy
   3 dead
   4 working

C 1 country code
   2 time difference
   3 international calling card
   4 behind
   5 ahead of

Conversation 1 통화 중 문제 발생 p.32   11.mp3

A: 소리가 끊겨서 부분적으로만 들리네요.
B: 뭐라고요?
A: 연결상태가 아주 좋지 않네요. 목소리가 울려서 거의 들리질 않습니다.
B: 그래요? 제 쪽은 잘 들리는데요. 그럼 제가 다시 걸겠습니다.
A: 제 배터리가 거의 다 됐어요. 이 얘기를 나중에 해도 될까요?
B: 그러죠. 언제 다시 전화 주시겠어요?
A: 목요일까지는 바빠요. 목요일 이후에 전화해 주시겠어요?
B: 좋아요. 금요일 오전 10시에 전화 드리겠습니다.

Conversation 2 국제전화 걸기 p.33   12.mp3

A: 린다씨, 국제 전화를 걸고 싶은데 몇 가지 물어볼게요.
B: 네, 말씀하세요.
A: 로마에 있는 폴에게 전화하고 싶은데, 거기는 몇 시인가요?
B: 로마는 현재 오전 5시 반입니다.
A: 그러면 네 시간 후에 전화 연결해 주시겠어요?
B: 네, 4시간 후에 폴에게 연결해 드리겠습니다.
A: 아, 그리고 분당 전화 요금이 얼마인지도 알려주세요.
B: 네, 1분당 1075원입니다.

Practice 1 Let's Speak p.34

A   1 ⓑ   2 ⓓ   3 ⓔ   4 ⓐ   5 ⓕ   6 ⓒ

B   1 it's 7 hours behind Seoul / Seoul is 7 hours ahead of Budapest
2 hear what you're saying / a bad connection / Let me speak louder then / hang up and call me again

Practice 2 Listen-up p.35

Audio Script – A, B   13.mp3

Jessica	Hello. Could I speak to Mr. Scott, please?
Mr. Scott	Speaking.
Jessica	Hello, Mr. Scott. This is Jessica Norman from Connections Telecom. I believe you left a message on my answering machine.

Mr. Scott	Hello, Ms. Norman. I have been waiting for your call.
Jessica	I'm sorry for calling you so late. Actually, I've just returned from a business trip.
Mr. Scott	That explains it. I didn't know about that.

제시카	여보세요. 스캇 씨와 통화할 수 있을까요?
스캇 씨	접니다.
제시카	안녕하세요, 스캇 씨. 커넥션스 텔레콤의 제시카 노먼입니다. 제 자동응답기에 메시지를 남기셨더군요.
스캇 씨	안녕하세요, 노먼 씨. 당신 전화를 기다리고 있었어요.
제시카	늦게 전화해서 죄송해요. 사실 방금 출장에서 돌아왔거든요.
스캇 씨	그랬군요. 몰랐어요.

Audio Script – C   14.mp3

A	Hello?
B	Hello. This is the operator from DDS. Would you like to accept a collect call from Mr. Peter Jackson?
A	Sure. I'll accept it. You can connect us.

A	여보세요?
B	안녕하십니까. DDS 사의 교환원입니다. 피터 잭슨 씨에게서 온 수신자 부담 전화를 받으시겠습니까?
A	네. 받을게요. 연결해 주세요.

A   1 The caller's name is Jessica Norman.
2 She works for Connections Telecom.
3 Because he was on his business trip.

B   1 speak to
2 Speaking
3 This / from
4 left a message
5 waiting for
6 calling you so late

C   1 F
2 F
3 T

WEEK 04 \ 미팅 약속 정하기

Vocabulary Check-up p.41

A 1 ⓓ 2 ⓒ 3 ⓔ 4 ⓐ 5 ⓑ

B 1 a rain-check
2 was held up
3 tied up
4 available

C 1 came up / make it
2 set a date
3 make it / later
4 was scheduled(supposed) to
5 good time

Conversation 1 약속 정하기 p.42   15.mp3

A: 여보세요? 토마스 씨와 통화할 수 있을까요? ICN사의 제인입니다.

B: 제인, 안녕하세요! 어떻게 지내세요?

A: 잘 지내요, 토마스 씨. 다음 미팅 날짜를 정했으면 하는데요. 언제가 좋으신 가요?

B: 수요일 2시쯤이 어떠세요?

A: 약속 잡기 전에 제 일정부터 확인해 볼게요.

B: 네, 기다리겠습니다.

A: 죄송하지만 그날은 안 되겠는데요. 대신 금요일은 어떠세요?

B: 네. 저도 좋습니다. 그럼 금요일에 뵙겠습니다.

Conversation 2 약속 다시 정하기 p.43   16.mp3

A: 여보세요, 데이비드입니다.

B: 안녕하세요, 제인입니다. 금요일에 우리가 술 한잔 하기로 했었는데요, 죄 송하지만 약속을 취소해야 할 것 같아요. 약속을 다시 잡을 수 있을까요?

A: 그래요. 언제가 좋으신지 알려 주세요.

B: 다음 주 월요일, 같은 시간에 어떠세요? 스케줄 괜찮으세요?

A: 네. 월요일은 저도 좋아요. 그럼 그때 봬요.

Practice 1 Let's Speak p.44

A 1 set / when
2 convenient / with
3 afraid / make / earlier
4 How / schedule like

B 1 I can't make it to our appointment on Monday.
2 Can we reschedule it?
3 Let me check my schedule first
4 Thursday is fine with me

Practice 2 Listen-up p.45

Audio Script – A, B   17.mp3

Mark | Hello, this is Mark Sanders speaking. May I talk with Julie Simpson?

Julie | This is Julie. What can I do for you, Mark?

Mark | I would really like to meet you sometime this week to talk to you about our new project. Are you available to get together this Thursday morning?

Julie | I'm sorry, but Thursday isn't good for me. I'll be out of the office all day. How about Friday afternoon instead?

Mark | Okay, I can do that. Is four o'clock an acceptable time?

Julie | It sounds perfect. I'm looking forward to seeing you.

마크 | 여보세요, 마크 샌더스입니다. 줄리 심슨 씨와 통화할 수 있을까요?

줄리 | 제가 줄리입니다. 무슨 용건인가요, 마크 씨?

마크 | 우리 프로젝트에 관해 논의하기 위해 이번 주중에 한번 만나 뵙고 싶습니다. 목 요일 오전에 모이는 게 가능하신가요?

줄리 | 죄송합니다만, 목요일은 안 돼요. 하루 종일 사무실을 비우거든요. 대신 금요일 오후는 어때요?

마크 | 좋아요, 가능해요. 4시 괜찮으세요?

줄리 | 좋습니다. 그때 뵙겠습니다.

Audio Script – C   18.mp3

A | Good morning, this is Brad Crawford. I'm sorry, but I'm going to have to cancel this morning's appointment.

B | Are you serious? But we really need to meet soon.

A | Yes, I know. But something important has come up. Why don't we reschedule our meeting?

B | Okay, how about later on today? I have time from one until the end of the day.

A | Hmm… I think I can be there by three thirty. Yeah, I can definitely make it then.

B | Excellent. I'll be here waiting for you to arrive then.

A | 안녕하세요, 브래드 크래포드입니다. 죄송합니다만, 오늘 아침의 약속을 취소해 야겠어요.

B | 정말요? 하지만 빨리 만나 봬야 하잖아요.

A | 네, 알아요. 하지만 중요한 일이 갑자기 생겼어요. 미팅 일정을 재조정하는 게 어 때요?

B | 좋아요, 오늘 오후는 어때요? 1시부터 오늘 퇴근 전까지 시간이 있어요.

A | 음…, 제가 거기로 3시 반까지 갈 수 있어요. 네, 충분히 갈 수 있습니다.

B | 좋아요. 그럼 여기서 기다리겠습니다.

A 1 T 2 F 3 T

B 1 May I talk with
2 This is
3 meet you sometime this week
4 Are you available
5 isn't good for me
6 out of the office
7 I'm looking forward to

C 1 He has to cancel his appointment.
2 Something important has come up.
3 They will meet at three thirty later that day.

WEEK 05 \ 출퇴근 인사와 휴가 신청

Vocabulary Check-up p.47

A 1 ⓓ 2 ⓑ 3 ⓔ 4 ⓐ 5 ⓒ

B 1 take off
2 get to work
3 coming down
4 was stuck in / late

C 1 tomorrow off
2 call in sick
3 cover for
4 call / a day
5 annual leave

Conversation 1 출근 인사 하기 p.48   19.mp3

A: 좋은 아침, 자넷! 오늘 어때요?
B: 안녕하세요, 좋아요. 당신은요?
A: 사실 좀 피곤해요. 어젯밤에 겨우 3시간밖에 못 잤거든요.
B: 왜요?
A: 새 프로젝트 때문에 연속 4일간 야근했거든요.
B: 안됐네요. 하지만 몸부터 돌봐야죠.
A: 하루 쉬었으면 좋겠어요.
B: 언제쯤 끝날 것 같은데요?
A: 확실하진 않지만, 아마도 끝마치려면 1주일이 더 걸릴 것 같아요.

Conversation 2 휴가 신청하기 p.49   20.mp3

A: 여보세요, 워커 씨, 제인입니다. 오늘 출근 못 한다고 말씀드리려고 전화 했습니다.
B: 병가를 내는 이유를 말해주겠어요?
A: 어젯밤 내내 몹시 아팠거든요. 일어날 때는 눈조차 뜰 수 없었어요.
B: 요즘 몸이 안 좋다고 들었는데 빨리 나아지길 바랍니다.
A: 감사합니다. 내일은 괜찮아질 겁니다. 좀 쉬면 될 거예요.
B: 그런데, 내일 있을 회의 준비는 다 됐습니까?
A: 거의요. 폴이 대신해주기로 했습니다.
B: 알겠어요. 몸조리 잘하세요.

Practice 1 Let's Speak p.50

A 1 ⓓ 2 ⓑ 3 ⓐ 4 ⓒ 5 ⓔ

B 1 to tell you that I can't come in today
2 why you are calling in sick
3 take a rest for a couple of days
4 I'll get better soon

Practice 2 Listen-up p.51

Audio Script – A, B   21.mp3

Kevin   Hey, welcome back to the office. How did you enjoy your vacation?
Linda   It was really relaxing. It felt so good to be able to get away from here for a while.
Kevin   That must have been nice.
Linda   So how have you been?
Kevin   I've been great. Everything is going well for me. Ah, while you were gone, you missed a lot of exciting things.
Linda   Really? What happened while I was away? Did anyone get fired?
Kevin   No, no one got fired. However, they posted a list of people getting promoted on the bulletin board. Your boss was one of them.

케빈   다시 출근한 걸 환영해요. 휴가는 어떻게 보냈어요?
린다   잘 쉬었어요. 잠시나마 여기서 벗어날 수 있어서 무척 좋았죠.
케빈   좋았겠군요.
린다   어떻게 지냈어요?
케빈   좋았어요. 모든 게 잘 풀리고 있어요. 참, 떠나 있는 동안 당신은 흥미로운 일들을 많이 놓쳤어요.
린다   정말요? 제가 없는 동안 무슨 일이 있었는데요? 누가 해고됐어요?
케빈   아뇨, 해고된 사람은 없어요. 하지만 게시판에 승진한 사람들 목록이 붙었거든요. 당신 상사도 그들 중 하나예요.

Audio Script – C   22.mp3

A   Jason, you don't look very good today. What's the matter with you?
B   I feel awful. I think I'm coming down with something.
A   In that case, you'd better leave early and go home soon. You've been working too much overtime lately. That's probably why you're sick.
B   You may be right, but I can't leave yet. I have to finish my report by lunchtime.
A   You really should take care of your health first, or you might get even more sick.
B   You're right. I think I'll go home now and try to finish this report tomorrow. I'm sure that my boss will understand.

A   제이슨, 오늘 안색이 안 좋아 보이네요. 무슨 일이에요?
B   괴로워요. 어딘가 병에 걸린 것 같아요.
A   그렇다면, 조퇴해서 일찍 집에 가는 게 좋겠네요. 근래에 너무 많이 야근하고 있잖아요. 그래서 아마도 아픈 것 같아요.

B 그럴지도 몰라요. 하지만 조퇴할 수가 없어요. 점심때까지 보고서를 마쳐야 하거든요.

A 건강 먼저 챙겨야죠, 안 그러면 더 아파질지도 몰라요.

B 맞아요. 지금 집에 가고 보고서는 내일 끝내야겠네요. 상사가 이해해 줄 거라 믿어요.

A 1 She was on vacation.
   2 A list of people getting promoted was posted on the bulletin board.
   3 He got promoted.

B 1 did you enjoy your vacation
   2 get away from here for a while
   3 how have you been
   4 Everything is going well for me
   5 Did anyone get fired
   6 getting promoted
   7 Your boss was one of them

C 1 T
   2 T
   3 F

WEEK 06 \ 감사와 격려 표현하기

Vocabulary Check-up p.53

A 1 ⓓ 2 ⓔ 3 ⓐ 4 ⓒ 5 ⓑ

B 1 appreciate
   2 cheer up
   3 regretted hearing
   4 express our condolences

C 1 sorry
   2 stick with it
   3 means
   4 Congratulations
   5 understand

Conversation 1 축하와 감사 p.54   23.mp3

A: 안녕하세요, 파커 씨, 와주셔서 감사합니다.

B: 초대해 줘서 고마워요. 이거 선물입니다.

A: 아, 아무것도 안 가져오셔도 되는데. 아, 와인이군요. 저 와인 정말 좋아해요. 고맙습니다.

B: 오, 천만에요. 대단한 건 아니지만 이런 걸 좋아하실 것 같았어요.

A: 아, 좋은 소식 들었습니다. 승진 축하해요.

B: 감사합니다.

A: 그럼 지금 직급이 어떻게 되시나요?

B: 전무이사입니다.

Conversation 2 위로와 격려 p.55   24.mp3

A: 주가가 폭락했다고 들었어요. 사업에 큰 영향을 끼쳤나요?

B: 네, 많은 문제를 일으켰어요.

A: 그거 안됐네요. 제 사업 역시 안 좋았어요.

B: 그렇지만 우리 둘 다 곧 나아질 거라 믿어요.

A: 네, 그렇죠. 단지 상황이 더 악화될까 봐 걱정돼요.

B: 그럴 수도 있겠죠. 하지만 긍정적으로 생각하도록 노력해 봅시다.

Practice 1 Let's Speak p.56

A 1 ⓒ 2 ⓐ 3 ⓑ 4 ⓓ

B 1 I Everything has been pretty difficult / I understand how you feel. / will turn around soon and get better
   2 regreted hearing the tragic news / express my condolences / I appreciate it.

Practice 2 Listen-up p.57

Audio Script – A, B   25.mp3

Ronald	Nancy, congratulations on your award. You must be so happy to be the salesperson of the year.
Nancy	Thanks so much. I really can't believe that I won this award.
Ronald	Why do you say that? You did a great job.
Nancy	Well, I couldn't have done it without the rest of my team. The award should go to everyone, not just one person.
Ronald	It's so considerate of you to say that.

로널드 낸시, 수상 축하해요. 올해의 영업사원이 되어서 기쁘시겠어요.

낸시 고맙습니다. 제가 이 상을 탔다는 게 정말 믿어지지 않아요.

로널드 왜 그런 말을 해요? 훌륭하게 잘 해냈잖아요.

낸시 저희 팀원들이 없었다면 불가능했을 거예요. 이 상은 저 한 사람에게만 아니라 모두에게 해당된다고 봐요.

로널드 그렇게 말씀하시다니 무척 사려 깊으시네요.

Audio Script – C   26.mp3

A	Patricia, what's the matter? You look upset about something.
B	My doctor just told me that I have a medical problem. I'm going to have to quit my job.
A	That's terrible. What exactly did he say the problem is?
B	He told me that I've got cancer.
A	I'm sure you're going to get better. Doctors can treat lots of types of cancer these days.
B	Thanks for the encouragement. I hope I get better.

A 패트리샤, 무슨 일이에요? 뭔가 기분이 안 좋아 보이는데요.

B 주치의가 그러는데 몸에 이상이 있대요. 일을 그만둬야 할 것 같아요.

A 저런. 정확히 문제가 뭐라고 그러던가요?

B 제가 암에 걸렸대요.

A 좋아질 거라 믿어요. 요즘에 의사들이 여러 종류의 암을 치료할 수 있잖아요.

B 격려해 줘서 고마워요. 저도 나아졌으면 좋겠네요.

A 1 F 2 T 3 T

B 1 congratulations on your award
2 be the salesperson
3 I won this award
4 should go to everyone
5 so considerate of you

C 1 She has cancer.
2 She is going to quit her job.
3 He says that doctors can treat many types of cancer nowadays.

PLUS WEEK \ 사무기기 다루기

Vocabulary Check-up p.59

A 1 ⓑ 2 ⓓ 3 ⓔ 4 ⓒ 5 ⓐ

B 1 got jammed
2 is infected with
3 not installed
4 out of toner

C 1 photocopy
2 start
3 be down
4 partition / reboot
5 tidy up

Conversation 1 컴퓨터 다루기 p.60   27.mp3

A: 컴퓨터가 가동되질 않아요. 부팅시키려 해봤는데 작동을 하지 않습니다. 제 컴퓨터가 바이러스에 감염된 것 같아요.

B: 최근에 바이러스 체크를 하셨나요?

A: 아뇨, 한 적 없어요.

B: 복구 USB를 사용해서 재부팅하는 대로 바이러스 프로그램을 실행해 보는 게 좋겠습니다. 아시겠죠?

A: 네, 해볼게요. 그건 그렇고, 오늘 있을 프레젠테이션 때문에 문서를 출력해서 복사해야 하는데, 프린터에 토너가 다 떨어졌더군요. 아직 교체되지 않았나요?

B: 잘 모르겠는데요. 여전히 토너가 떨어져 있으면 총무부에서 새 카트리지를 받아 오셔야 합니다.

Conversation 2 복사기 다루기 p.61   28.mp3

A: 무슨 일이에요?

B: 서버가 다운되더니 지금은 복사기에 종이까지 걸렸어요. 그런데 어떻게 빼내야 하는지 모르겠어요.

A: 정말 운이 안 좋은 날인 것 같네요. 어디 봅시다…. 먼저 이 덮개를 열고 나서 이 부분을 밀어서 빼내야 합니다. 그러고 나서 그 부분의 뚜껑을 열어요. 아, 종이가 보이네요. 그럼 걸린 종이를 빼내세요.

B: 도와주셔서 감사합니다. 이걸 고칠 사람을 부르려면 누구에게 연락해야 하는지 몰랐거든요.

A: 별말씀을요. 제가 기계를 잘 다루는 편이거든요. 도움이 필요하시면 말씀하세요.

Practice 1 Let's Speak p.62

A 1 ⓒ
2 ⓓ
3 ⓑ
4 ⓐ

B 1 Internet access has been bad the entire day / exactly sure what is wrong / with Internet access in my department
2 install this software on my computer first / insert the flash drive into the computer / start installing automatically

Practice 2 Listen-up p.63

Audio Script – A, B   29.mp3

Laura　Do you think you can give me a hand here? I don't know how to use the fax machine.

Daniel　Okay, it's really simple. First, put the paper that you want to fax into the tray here.

Laura　That's easy. Then what should I do?

Daniel　Next, input the number that you're sending it to. The fax should dial the number automatically.

Laura　Okay, I can hear a ringing sound right now. Oh, what's that horrible noise?

Daniel　That's the sound of the fax machine connecting. Now, your paper will automatically go through the machine, and your fax will be sent.

로라　저 좀 도와줄 수 있어요? 이 팩스 기기를 어떻게 사용하는 건지 모르겠어요.

다니엘　네, 간단해요. 먼저, 보내려는 종이를 종이함에 넣으세요.

로라　쉽네요. 그런 다음 뭘 해야 하죠?

다니엘　그다음, 팩스 보내는 곳의 번호를 입력하세요. 팩스 기기가 자동으로 그 번호로 전화를 걸 거예요.

로라　그렇군요. 지금 울리는 소리가 나는데, 이 시끄러운 소리는 뭐죠?

다니엘　팩스 기기가 연결되는 소리예요. 이제 종이가 자동으로 기기를 통과하고, 팩스가 갈 거예요.

Audio Script – C   30.mp3

A　Sylvia, do you mind if I ask you for a favor?

B　Well, I'm kind of busy right now, so I can't do anything for you.

A　Oh, it's not that. I'd just like to borrow your stapler. Mine ran out of staples earlier today.

B　Of course you can borrow it. Here you are. Do you need anything else?

A　Well, if it's all right with you, could you lend me a couple of pens, please?

B　That's not a problem. You can keep them. You don't have to give them back to me.

A 실비아, 뭐 좀 부탁해도 될까요?

B 음, 지금 좀 바빠서 도와줄 수가 없겠는데요.

A 아, 그런 건 아니고요. 스테이플러를 빌리고 싶어서요. 스테이플러 심이 오늘 아침에 떨어져서요.

B 그럼요, 빌려줄 수 있어요. 여기요. 또 필요한 거 있어요?

A 음, 괜찮다면 펜 좀 몇 개 빌릴 수 있을까요?

B 그럼요. 가지세요. 돌려주지 않아도 돼요.

A 1 F   2 F   3 T

B 1 how to use the fax machine
2 put the paper that you want to fax
3 input the number that you're sending it to
4 will automatically go through

C 1 He wants to borrow her stapler.
2 He is out of staples.
3 She gives him a couple of pens.

PART 3 \ 방문객 맞이하기
Welcoming Visitors

WEEK 07 \ 공항에서 손님 맞이하기

Vocabulary Check-up p.69

A 1 ⓓ
2 ⓔ
3 ⓒ
4 ⓑ
5 ⓐ

B 1 booked a room
2 pick / up
3 give / a hand
4 make a reservation

C 1 layover(stopover)
2 first visit
3 give / a ride
4 aren't you
5 was delayed

Conversation 1 방문객 맞이하기 p.70   31.mp3

A: 리처드슨 씨 맞죠? 제 이름은 캐롤, 캐롤 그린입니다. 일전에 전화 통화한 적 있어요?

B: 네, 그린 씨, 안녕하세요?

A: 예. 마침내 만나 뵙게 되어 정말 반갑습니다. 한국으로의 여행은 어떠셨어요?

B: 나쁘지 않았어요. 그런데 정말 장시간의 비행이었어요.

A: 네, 시차에 적응하려면 시간이 좀 걸릴 겁니다. 제가 호텔까지 태워 드릴게요. 가방 하나는 제가 들겠습니다.

B: 고맙습니다. 호텔이 회의장과 가까운가요?

A: 네, 그렇습니다. 그래서 편하실 겁니다.

B: 잘 됐군요.

Conversation 2 공항에서 호텔까지 p.71   32.mp3

A: 한국에는 처음 오셨나요?

B: 네, 마음이 들뜨는군요. 그런데 호텔이 여기서 먼가요?

A: 아니요, 여기서 30분 이상 안 걸릴 겁니다. 블루릿지 호텔이 편리해서 블루릿지 호텔을 예약해 두었습니다. 마음에 드셨으면 좋겠네요.

B: 잘됐네요. 고맙습니다.

A: 그럼, 일이 시작되기 전에 호텔에서 시간 갖고 쉬십시오.

B: 좋아요. 샤워하고 나서 귀사로 출발하겠습니다.

Practice 1 Let's Speak p.72

A 1 ⓒ
2 ⓕ
3 ⓑ
4 ⓔ
5 ⓓ
6 ⓐ

B 1 I booked a room at the Hyatt Hotel. (I made a reservation for the Hyatt Hotel.) / you don't mind the Hyatt Hotel / get changed to something more comfortable then
2 take long to get to the hotel / you can take a shower or get some rest / head out to our company / very thoughtful of you

Practice 2 Listen-up p.73

Audio Script – A, B   33.mp3

Nancy	Mr. Davis? My name is Nancy, Nancy Brown. We've spoken on the phone before.
Mr. Davis	Ah, Ms. Brown. It's very nice to finally meet you.
Nancy	The pleasure is all mine. Please call me Nancy. So did you enjoy the flight?
Mr. Davis	Yes, but I'm still a bit jet-lagged.

Nancy	Right. I hope you will feel better soon. This way, Mr. Davis. There's a car waiting for us outside.
Mr. Davis	Is the Hilton Hotel far from your company?
Nancy	It just takes about 5 minutes by car, but the convention center is a little far from the hotel. But don't worry. I'll give you a ride whenever you need to go during your stay.
Mr. Davis	That's very kind of you. Thank you.

낸시	데이비스 씨? 제 이름은 낸시, 낸시 브라운입니다. 일전에 전화로 통화한 적 있죠?
데이비드 씨	아, 브라운 씨. 이렇게 마침내 만나게 돼서 반갑네요.
낸시	저도 반갑습니다. 낸시라고 불러주세요. 비행은 괜찮으셨나요?
데이비드 씨	네, 그런데 아직은 시차로 좀 피곤하네요.
낸시	그렇죠. 빨리 좋아지시길 바라요. 이쪽으로 오세요, 데이비스 씨. 밖에 저희를 위해 차가 대기하고 있습니다.
데이비드 씨	힐튼 호텔이 당신 회사에서 먼가요?
낸시	차로 5분밖에 안 걸려요. 하지만 컨벤션 센터는 호텔에서 약간 멉니다. 하지만 걱정하지 마세요. 머무시는 동안 가실 일이 있을 때마다 차로 모셔다 드리겠습니다.
데이비드 씨	정말 친절하시군요. 고맙습니다.

A 1 F 2 T 3 F 4 T

B 1 My name is
2 It's very nice
3 is all mine
4 enjoy the flight
5 a bit of jet-lagged
6 waiting for us
7 far from your company
8 just takes about 5 minutes
9 I'll give you a ride

WEEK 08 \ 비즈니스 미팅 준비하기

Vocabulary Check-up p.75

A 1 ⓒ
2 ⓔ
3 ⓓ
4 ⓐ
5 ⓑ

B 1 timeframe
2 on schedule
3 behind schedule
4 out of

C 1 are scheduled to
2 There / change
3 itinerary
4 This is
5 feel free

Conversation 1 일정 확인하기 p.76   34.mp3

A: 박람회 일정은 어떻게 됩니까?

B: 저희 부장님께서 박람회 행사 일정을 짜느라 애쓰고 계십니다. 최종 일정이 정해지면, 미리 알려 드리겠습니다.

A: 고맙습니다. 빠듯한 일정으로 그 많은 것들을 하시니 정말 바쁘신 것 같네요.

B: 맞습니다. 일정표를 확인해 보고 공장 견학이 몇 시에 예정되어 있는지 확인해 볼게요. 아, 일정보다 이르니, 원하시면 잠깐 쉬셔도 됩니다. 일정상 한 시간 정도 여유가 있거든요.

A: 휴식이라니 반갑네요. 커피 한 잔 할 수 있겠군요.

Conversation 2 다른 사람 소개하기 p.77   35.mp3

A: 안녕하세요, 피오나 씨. 어떻게 지내세요?

B: 잘 지냅니다. 고마워요. 스펜서 씨, 이쪽은 제 동료 카덴입니다. 저희는 같은 시기에 입사했지만 카덴 씨가 선임이에요. 서울로 오시기 전에 제주 지사에서 근무하셨어요.

A: 안녕하세요, 카덴 씨. 스펜서라고 불러주세요.

C: 안녕하세요, 스펜서 씨. 만나서 반갑습니다.

A: 저도 반갑습니다. 명함이 다 떨어졌군요. 다음에 드려도 될까요?

C: 그럼요. 여기 제 명함입니다.

A: 고맙습니다.

Practice 1 Let's Speak p.78

A 1 ⓐ 2 ⓒ 3 ⓑ 4 ⓓ

B 1 discuss today's schedule before we leave / We'll be leaving here by car at 10:00 / scheduled to be back here by 5:00
2 we should postpone the visit until next week / has the schedule been changed / due to that major thunderstorm

Practice 2 Listen-up p.79

Audio Script – A, B   36.mp3

Mark	I don't think you've met Ms. Maura. She's one of our clients, and she's from Spain. She's come to our head office to see how we maintain our production line.
Dongsu	Hello, Ms. Maura. I'm Dongsu Jeong. Please call me Dongsu.
Ms. Maura	Hello, Dongsu. My name is Patricia Maura, but my English-speaking friends call me Pat. So you can call me Pat.
Dongsu	Oh, that sounds easier for me. So, how was your flight? Did you come from Barcelona?
Ms. Maura	No, from Madrid. Have you been there?
Dongsu	No, but I'd love to go there one day.
Ms. Maura	Good. It's a nice place. I think you will like it there.
Dongsu	Great. Here's my business card.

마크	마우라 씨를 전에 만난 적 없으시죠? 저희 고객 중 한 분으로, 스페인에서 오셨습니다. 우리의 생산라인이 어떻게 유지되는지 보러 저희 본사에 오셨습니다.
동수	안녕하세요, 마우라 씨. 저는 정동수입니다. 동수라고 불러주세요.
마우라 씨	안녕하세요, 동수 씨. 제 이름은 패트리샤 마우라입니다만, 영어권 친구들이 부르듯 팻이라고 불러주세요.
동수	아, 그게 편하겠네요. 그리고, 비행은 어떠셨나요? 바르셀로나에서 오신 건가요?
마우라 씨	아뇨, 마드리드에서 왔습니다. 가보신 적 있나요?
동수	없습니다, 하지만 언젠가 가보고 싶군요.
마우라 씨	그래요. 그곳은 정말 멋집니다. 맘에 드실 거예요.
동수	그렇군요. 여기 제 명함입니다.

A
1 to see how they maintain their production line
2 Pat
3 Madrid, Spain

B
1 you've met
2 call me Dongsu
3 my English-speaking friends call me Pat
4 how was your flight
5 Have you been there
6 my business card

WEEK 09 \ 회사 소개와 공장 견학

Vocabulary Check-up p.81

A 1 ⓒ 2 ⓐ 3 ⓓ 4 ⓑ 5 ⓔ

B
1 was founded in
2 good reputation
3 look around
4 is based in

C
1 company history
2 workshop
3 branches
4 gross profit
5 in three shifts

Conversation 1 회사 소개하기 p.82   37.mp3

A: 귀사에 관해 설명해 주시겠습니까?
B: 네. 저희 회사는 1971년에 설립되었고, 대략 25만 명의 직원이 있습니다.
A: 총수익은 얼마나 됩니까?
B: 연간 1억5천만 달러 이상의 총수익을 올리고 있습니다.
A: 한 가지 더 질문할게요. 본사는 어디에 있습니까?
B: 인천에 있어요. 서울 근교입니다.
A: 그거 흥미롭군요. 본사는 서울에 있을 줄 알았는데요.
B: 여러 가지 이유로 그곳에 있는데요. 그 중 하나는 항구가 사무실과 가까워서 더 쉽고 효율적으로 선적을 관리할 수 있다는 점입니다.

Conversation 2 공장 견학하기 p.83   38.mp3

A: 지금까지 본사를 보셨으니, 이제 저희 작업장을 안내해 드리겠습니다. 견학 내내 설명해 드리겠지만, 도중에 질문이 있으시면 언제든 해주십시오. 작업 현장을 보러 가실까요?
B: 앞서 가시죠.
A: 이곳이 저희의 주 작업실입니다. 여기서 주요 뼈대를 제작합니다. 이곳엔 200명 이상의 정규직원과 100명의 시간제 근무직원이 있는데, 다른 착취 공장과는 다르게 3교대로 일합니다.
B: 그렇다면 직원들을 과도하게 근무시키지 않겠군요.
A: 말씀드리고 싶은 게 많은데요, 그 중 하나는 저희 제품의 질과 섬세함, 그리고 직원들의 사기가 충만하다는 것을 자랑으로 여긴다는 점입니다.
B: 그거 정말 멋진데요. 제가 여기서 일하고 싶네요!

Practice 1 Let's Speak p.84

A
1 ⓐ
2 ⓓ
3 ⓑ
4 ⓒ
5 ⓔ

B
1 was founded in 1971 / approximately half million employees / a gross profit of over $70 million per annum / It's based in Washington
2 the second largest sports shoe manufacturer / What is your market share? / it was over 35 percent last year

Practice 2 Listen-up p.85

Audio Script – A, B   39.mp3

Mr. Hills	Good morning, Ms. Simmons. I'm glad you made it here today.
Ms. Simmons	It's good to see you, Mr. Hills. So, what are you going to show me this morning?
Mr. Hills	I'm taking you on a tour of our company. This will let you see firsthand what we do here.
Ms. Simmons	Okay. What are we going to do first?
Mr. Hills	I thought we would visit the factory floor first. You can look at how we manufacture our products.
Ms. Simmons	That sounds good. What products do you make here?
Mr. Hills	At this location, we manufacture lots of small electronic parts. We ship them to numerous other places overseas as well as within the country.

힐스 씨	안녕하세요, 시먼스 씨. 오늘 이곳으로 모시게 되어 기쁩니다.
시먼스 씨	뵙게 돼서 반가워요, 힐스 씨. 자, 오늘 아침에는 어디를 보여주실 건가요?
힐스 씨	저희 회사 견학을 시켜드릴 건데요. 여기서 저희가 뭘 하는지 직접 확인하실 수 있을 겁니다.

시먼스 씨 좋아요. 저희는 먼저 뭘 하나요?

힐스 씨 먼저 공장 작업장을 방문할 것 같습니다. 어떻게 제품을 제조하는지 보실 수 있어요.

시먼스 씨 그거 좋군요. 여기서 어떤 제품을 만드나요?

힐스 씨 여기서는, 여러 작은 전자부품들을 제조합니다. 국내뿐만 아니라 해외 여기저기로 선적하죠.

A 1 F
2 T
3 F

B 1 you made it here today
2 on a tour of our company
3 at how we manufacture
4 At this location
5 as well as within the country

PLUS WEEK \ 한국 문화 소개하기

Vocabulary Check-up p.87

A 1 ⓑ
2 ⓐ
3 ⓔ
4 ⓓ
5 ⓒ

B 1 join / for dinner
2 well-known
3 have a drink / free
4 have any plans

C 1 taking a night tour
2 tourist attraction
3 spicy
4 vegetarian dishes
5 old place

Conversation 1 한국음식 소개하기 p.88 40.mp3

A: 미셸 씨, 안 바쁘시면 저희와 함께 저녁식사 하시겠어요?

B: 좋죠. 고마워요.

A: 불고기 드셔보셨어요?

B: 아뇨, 못 먹어봤어요. 어떤 음식인지 설명해 주실래요?

A: 얇게 저며서 양념한 고기예요. 외국인들 사이에서 인기 있어요.

B: 좋아요. 한번 먹어볼게요. 술도 마실 건가요?

A: 아, 아마 소주 한두 잔 정도는 먹을 것 같아요. 하지만 우리 일행 중 술 많이 먹는 사람은 없으니 걱정하지 마세요.

B: 네, 안심되는군요.

Conversation 2 관광지 추천하기 p.89 41.mp3

A: 이후에 무슨 계획 있으세요?

B: 아니요, 호텔로 돌아가서 쉬려고요.

A: 그러면, 한국음식을 맛보셨으니, 이 근처에 있는 한국 관광지에 가보는 게 어때요?

B: 좋죠. 추천할 만한 곳이 있어요?

A: 종로에 외국 방문객들에게 인기가 높은 인사동이 있습니다. 인사동에서 한국의 전통 문화를 경험해 보실 수 있어요. 한국의 그림, 수공예품, 전통의상, 도자기 등요.

B: 재미있을 것 같네요. 거기서 기념품도 살 수 있겠군요.

A: 좋습니다! 어두워지기 전에 서두릅시다.

Practice 1 Let's Speak p.90

A 1 ⓒ
2 ⓑ
3 ⓓ
4 ⓔ
5 ⓐ

B 1 I haven't made any plans
2 take you out to dinner
3 rice with a mixture of vegetables
4 I'd love to try it

Practice 2 Listen-up p.91

Audio Script – A, B 42.mp3

The host	So, how did you like our Korean traditional food?
Visitor	It was great. I love having variety when it comes to food. Thank you for inviting me out to dinner.
The host	I'm glad that you enjoyed everything.
Visitor	Wow, is that the time? I've got to be going. Thank you again for the lovely dinner. I've really enjoyed talking with you as well.
The host	I hope we can stay in touch.

접대자 그럼. 한국 전통 음식은 어떠셨나요?

방문객 훌륭했어요. 음식은 다양하게 먹는 걸 좋아하거든요. 저녁 식사에 초대해 주셔서 감사합니다.

접대자 마음에 드셨다니 다행입니다.

방문객 와, 시간이 벌써 이렇게 됐나요? 가봐야겠군요. 멋진 저녁식사 다시 한번 감사드립니다. 대화도 정말 즐거웠어요.

접대자 계속 연락하고 지냈으면 합니다.

Audio Script – C   43.mp3

The host	It looks like our work here is all finished.
Client	That's great. Now, I've got a couple of days to see the sights around Seoul.
The host	Where are you planning to go? Do you have anything in mind?
Client	Not really. This is my first visit to Korea. Do you have any recommendations for me?
The host	Sure. You should check out *Gyeongbokgung*. It's a palace from the Chosun Dynasty. And you should also visit Insadong to learn about traditional Korean culture.
Client	Okay, those two places sound really good. Do you have any more recommendations?
The host	Well, you might want to visit the Korean Folk Village in Yongin. It's about one hour south of here, but it's really nice.
Client	Thanks a lot for your advice.

접대자	이쯤 해서 우리 일은 모두 끝난 것 같습니다.
고객	좋군요. 이제 2~3일 정도 서울을 관광하려고 해요.
접대자	어디를 가볼 계획이세요? 생각해 둔 곳 있으세요?
고객	그렇진 않아요. 이번이 한국 첫 방문이거든요. 추천할 만한 곳 있어요?
접대자	그럼요. 경복궁은 가보셔야 해요. 조선시대 궁궐이에요. 그리고 한국 전통문화에 대해 알려면 인사동을 가보셔야 하고요.
고객	알겠습니다. 이 두 군데는 정말 좋을 것 같군요. 다른 추천지도 있으세요?
접대자	음, 용인에 있는 한국 민속촌도 가볼 만합니다. 여기서 남쪽으로 한 시간 정도 걸리는데, 정말 멋져요.
고객	알려 주셔서 정말 고맙습니다.

A 1 T 2 T 3 F

B 1 how did you like
2 Thank you for inviting me
3 got to be going
4 enjoyed talking with you

C 1 It is her first visit to Korea.
2 to *Gyeongbokgung* and Insadong
3 the Korean Folk Village in Yongin

PART 4 해외 출장
Business Trip

WEEK 10 \ 공항 이용하기

Vocabulary Check-up p.97

A 1 ⓐ 2 ⓔ 3 ⓑ 4 ⓒ 5 ⓓ

B 1 confirm my reservation
2 book a ticket
3 check / in
4 fill out

C 1 window seat
2 return ticket
3 round-trip ticket
4 legroom
5 carry-on luggage

Conversation 1 탑승 수속하기 p.98   44.mp3

A: 티켓을 보여주시겠습니까?
B: 여기요.
A: 런던행 대한항공 730기군요.
B: 네, 맞습니다.
A: 탑승 수속할 짐이 있으신가요, 김 선생님?
B: 네, 있어요. 이 가방 두 개를 체크인하고 싶습니다.
A: 알겠습니다. 창가 쪽 좌석을 원하십니까, 통로 쪽 좌석을 원하십니까?

B: 창가 쪽 좌석이 더 좋겠습니다.
A: 네. 좌석 35B를 드릴게요. 여기 탑승권 받으세요.

Conversation 2 세관 통과하기 p.99   45.mp3

A: 여권을 보여주시겠습니까?
B: 네, 그러죠.
A: 방문 목적이 무엇입니까?
B: 출장입니다.
A: 런던에 얼마나 머무실 계획이신가요?
B: 일주일 정도요.
A: 어디에 묵으실 겁니까?
B: GK 호텔에 머물 겁니다.
A: 알겠습니다. 즐거운 방문 되세요.
B: 고맙습니다.

Practice 1 Let's Speak p.100

A 1 ⓒ 2 ⓓ 3 ⓑ 4 ⓐ 5 ⓕ 6 ⓔ

B 1 confirm my reservation for the flight / have your name and destination
2 What's the purpose of your visit? / How long are you planning to stay / Where will you be staying?

Practice 2 Listen-up p.101

Audio Script – A, B 46.mp3

Client	I'd like to exchange some Korean won for dollars.
Changer	Okay. How much are you changing, sir?
Client	I need about $1,500. What's the exchange rate?
Changer	It's 1290 won per dollar. And there's a 1 percent fee.
Client	I see.
Changer	How would you like your money, sir?
Client	Could I have $1,000 in traveler's checks and $500 in cash, please?
Changer	Certainly. Please wait a moment.

고객	원화를 달러로 바꾸고 싶습니다.
환전원	네. 얼마를 환전하실 건가요?
고객	1,500달러요. 환율이 어떻게 돼요?
환전원	1달러당 1290원이에요. 그리고 1퍼센트의 수수료가 붙습니다.
고객	알겠습니다.
환전원	돈을 어떻게 드릴까요?
고객	현금으로 1000달러 주세요.
환전원	네. 잠시만 기다려주세요.

Audio Script – C 47.mp3

Traveler	Excuse me. My suitcase hasn't arrived yet. I've been waiting at least an hour at the luggage carousel, but I still haven't seen my bags.
Airport staff	I see. Did you have your name on your name tag?
Traveler	Yes, I had my name, address, and even my phone number on it.
Airport staff	Let me see. Could you give me a minute so that I can look for it?

여행객	실례합니다. 제 여행가방이 아직 도착하지 않았어요. 수하물 컨베이어에서 한 시간째 기다리고 있는데, 제 가방은 여전히 보이질 않아요.
공항 직원	알겠습니다. 이름표에 성함을 적어두셨습니까?
여행객	네, 제 이름과 주소, 그리고 전화번호까지 적어뒀습니다.
공항 직원	알아보죠. 찾아보겠습니다. 잠시만 기다려주시겠습니까?

A 1 F 2 T 3 F 4 T

B 1 How much are you changing
2 What's the exchange rate
3 How would you like
4 Could I have

C 4 - 1 – 3 - 5 - 2
Q: She lost her bags.

WEEK 11 \ 교통수단 이용하기

Vocabulary Check-up p.103

A 1 ⓑ 2 ⓓ 3 ⓒ 4 ⓔ 5 ⓐ

B 1 Go straight
2 go down / turn left
3 get off
4 reserved

C 1 across from
2 take me
3 near here
4 return the car
5 transfer to

Conversation 1 길 묻기 p.104 48.mp3

A: 트윈 타워 빌딩에 가는 방법을 말씀해 주시겠어요?
B: 네, 이 길을 따라 직진하셔서 세 번째 골목에서 왼쪽으로 꺾으세요. 그다음, 병원이 보일 때까지 길을 따라 올라가세요. 그 왼쪽 코통이로 돌아가시면 오른쪽에 트윈 타워 빌딩이 보일 겁니다.
A: 고맙습니다. 그런데 그곳으로 가는 더 쉬운 방법이 있나요?
B: 택시를 타도 되는데, 걸어갈 수 있는 거리에 있어요.
A: 알겠습니다. 말해주실 수 있는 대표 건물 같은 게 있나요?
B: 네, 그 주변에 서울 시청이 있습니다. 트윈 타워 빌딩 바로 옆에 있어요.

Conversation 2 자동차 렌트하기 p.105 49.mp3

A: 차를 렌트하고 싶습니다.
B: 생각하고 계신 특정 브랜드가 있으세요?
A: 그런 건 아니지만 소형차를 찾고 있습니다.
B: 알겠습니다. 남아있는 차가 어떤 게 있는지 한번 볼게요. 시보레 코발트가 있네요.
A: 렌트 비용이 얼마인가요?
B: 하루에 100달러입니다. 보험 포함이고요. 얼마 동안 렌트하실 건가요?
A: 3일 동안이요. 어디까지 보장되는 보험인가요?
B: 종합 보험입니다. 운전 면허증을 주시겠습니까?
A: 네. 여기요.

Practice 1 Let's Speak p.106

A 1 ⓐ
2 ⓒ
3 ⓓ
4 ⓔ
5 ⓕ
6 ⓑ

B 1 Which bus do I have to take / How many stops do I have to go / get off at the third stop
2 can you tell me how to get to / until you see the second traffic light / turn left and walk two blocks

Practice 2 Listen-up p.107

Audio Script – A, B 50.mp3

Customer	I'd like to rent a car.
Assistant	What type of car would you like?
Customer	I want an economy car.
Assistant	I'm sorry, we're all out of economy cars now.
Customer	Then, I'll take a mid-sized car.
Assistant	All right. May I have your driver's license and credit card?
Customer	Here you are. How much is the rate?
Assistant	It's 26 dollars a day plus tax. Would you like to buy optional insurance?
Customer	No, I'll take full coverage.

손님	차를 렌트하고 싶습니다.
점원	어떤 차종을 원하세요?
손님	소형차로 주세요.
점원	죄송하지만, 현재 소형차는 다 나가고 없습니다.
손님	그럼 중형차로 할게요.
점원	좋습니다. 운전면허증과 신용카드를 주시겠어요.
손님	여기요. 요금은 얼마인가요?
점원	세금 포함해서 하루에 26달러입니다. 선택 보험에 드시겠습니까?
손님	아뇨, 종합 보험으로 할게요.

A 1 a mid-sized car
2 her driver's license and credit card
3 comprehensive insurance
4 26 dollars

B 1 rent a car
2 we're all out of economy cars
3 May I have
4 How much is the rate
5 I'll take full coverage

WEEK 12 \ 무역박람회 참가하기

Vocabulary Check-up p.109

A 1 ⓒ
2 ⓐ
3 ⓑ
4 ⓔ
5 ⓓ

B 1 extra brochures
2 benefits
3 high demand
4 newly developed

C 1 show me
2 with / warranty
3 selling points

4 give / some information
5 answer any questions

Conversation 1 행사 참석하기 p.110 51.mp3

A: 회의 참관인으로 왔습니다.

B: 네. 신분증을 주시겠습니까? 모든 방문객이 기록되어야 합니다.

A: 그래요. 여기 있습니다.

B: 네⋯, 여기 신분증을 돌려드리겠습니다. 이 가방에는 저희의 기념품 꾸러미가 들어 있습니다. 그 꾸러미 안에 회의장 지도가 들어 있을 테니 가시는 길을 찾으실 수 있습니다. 또한, 회사 정보가 함께 수록된 참가 회사 목록이 들어 있습니다.

A: 고맙습니다. 여분의 브로셔를 더 받아갈 수 있을까요? 동료들과 나눠 가지려고요.

B: 물론이에요. 여기 있습니다. 필요한 게 있으시면 말씀해 주세요.

Conversation 2 제품 소개하기 p.111 52.mp3

A: 그 장치는 무엇에 쓰는 것인지 말씀해 주시겠어요?

B: 저희가 작은 거인이라 부르는 제품입니다. 겉보기에는 일반 배터리처럼 보이죠. 하지만 저희 제품의 최대 장점은 충전 없이 한 달간 쓸 수 있다는 겁니다.

A: 보증 기간이 얼마나 되죠?

B: 이 제품은 2년간 보증됩니다.

A: 이 장치를 제 휴대전화에 장착하는 방법을 다시 보여주시겠어요?

B: 네. 쉽습니다. 기꺼이 다시 보여드리지요.

Practice 1 Let's Speak p.112

A 1 ⓑ
2 ⓐ
3 ⓒ
4 ⓔ
5 ⓓ

B 1 This is our new model. / more economical and efficient compared to the competition / Could you show me how it works?
2 what this device is for / One of the advantages of this product is that / be possible to get a brochure

Practice 2 Listen-up p.113

Audio Script – A, B 53.mp3

Receptionist	Good morning.
Visitor	Good morning. I've pre-registered, and this is my confirmation slip.
Receptionist	Let me see. You're Mr. Steven Johnson?
Visitor	Yes, I am.
Receptionist	Okay. Here is your name tag. Please be sure to wear it in the trade show hall.
Visitor	I will.

Receptionist	Here's our welcoming bag. The map of the hall, the show program, the list of participants, and other materials… They're all in it.
Visitor	Thank you. May we take pictures at the exhibition?
Receptionist	In principle, no. But some of the exhibitors may let you. I suggest you inquire at each booth.

접수자	안녕하십니까.
참관인	안녕하세요. 사전 등록을 했고요, 이건 확인증입니다.
접수자	네. 스티븐 존슨 씨세요?
참관인	네, 그렇습니다.
접수자	좋습니다. 여기 명찰 받으세요. 무역박람회장에서 착용해 주세요.
참관인	그럴게요.
접수자	여기 저희가 준비한 가방을 드릴게요. 박람회장의 지도, 박람회의 프로그램, 참가자들 목록, 그리고 다른 자료들 등이 거기에 모두 담겨 있습니다.
참관인	감사합니다. 전시회에서 사진을 찍어도 될까요?
접수자	원칙적으로 안 됩니다. 하지만 일부 전시사들은 허락할 수도 있습니다. 각 부스에서 문의해 보시기 바랍니다.

A 1 F
2 F
3 T
4 T

B 1 I've pre-registered
2 Here is your name tag
3 be sure to wear it
4 the list of participants, and other materials
5 May we take pictures
6 I suggest you inquire

PLUS WEEK \ 호텔 & 레스토랑 이용하기

Vocabulary Check-up p.115

A 1 ⓓ
2 ⓔ
3 ⓒ
4 ⓐ
5 ⓑ

B 1 check in
2 single / double
3 vacancies
4 pay with / take Visa

C 1 room rate
2 ready
3 appetizer
4 How / like
5 recommend

Conversation 1 호텔 체크인하기 p.116   54.mp3

A: 오늘 묵을 빈방이 있나요?
B: 네, 있습니다. 얼마나 머무실 예정이신가요?
A: 4일간 머물 계획입니다.
B: 1인실을 원하십니까, 2인실을 원하십니까?
A: 2인실 부탁합니다. 발코니가 있는 흡연실로 주시겠어요?
B: 알겠습니다. 다른 것은요?
A: 1박에 얼마죠?
B: 250달러입니다.
A: 조식이 포함된 건가요?
B: 그렇습니다. 숙박카드 작성해 주세요.

Conversation 2 식당에서 주문하기 p.117   55.mp3

A: 지금 주문하시겠습니까?
B: 네, 음… 어떤 요리를 추천해 주시겠어요?
A: 오늘의 특별요리는 하우스 와인 한 잔과 함께 나오는 프라임 립입니다. 오늘만 특별 가격인 54달러에 드립니다.
B: 그럼 오늘의 특별요리로 할게요.
A: 잘 선택하셨습니다. 스테이크를 어떻게 요리해 드릴까요?
B: 중간보다 더 익혀서 주세요. 그리고 시저 샐러드도 주세요.
A: 알겠습니다. 음료수도 드시겠습니까?
B: 그냥 물 주세요.

Practice 1 Let's Speak p.118

A 1 ⓐ
2 ⓓ
3 ⓒ
4 ⓑ
5 ⓔ

B 1 I'd like to check in / Do you have a reservation / to take your bag
2 I'd like to reserve a room / What type of room / two double beds

Practice 2 Listen-up p.119

Audio Script – A, B   56.mp3

Waitress	Good evening. Do you have a reservation?
Guest	Yes, we have a table reserved for 7 o'clock.
Waitress	What's the name, sir?
Guest	It's Robert Park.
Waitress	Ah, yes. This way, please.
…	
Waitress	May I take your order?
Guest	What's today's special?
Waitress	Today's special is the sirloin steak. It comes with a salad, and roast potatoes as well.

Guest	I'll take it, please.
Waitress	An excellent choice! How would you like your steak?
Guest	I'd like it medium rare, please.

웨이트리스	어서오십시오. 예약하셨나요?
손님	네, 7시에 예약했습니다.
웨이트리스	성함이 어떻게 되시죠?
손님	로버트 박입니다.
웨이트리스	아, 네. 이쪽으로 오십시오.
...	
웨이트리스	주문하시겠습니까?
손님	오늘의 특별요리가 뭔가요?
웨이트리스	오늘의 특별요리는 채끝 스테이크입니다. 샐러드와 구운 감자도 같이 나옵니다.
손님	그걸로 할게요.
웨이트리스	잘 선택 하셨습니다! 스테이크는 어떻게 요리해 드릴까요?
손님	약간 덜 익혀서 주세요.

Audio Script – C
57.mp3

Guest	Sorry to trouble you, but I was wondering if you could help me. Would it be possible for me to extend my check-out time and settle my bill later today? Apparently, my flight has changed, so it's leaving tonight.
Receptionist	How late will it be?
Guest	Maybe another 3 hours. So it will be 3 o'clock when I check out.
Receptionist	I think we can help you with that.
Guest	That would be great. I appreciate it.

손님	번거롭게 해서 죄송한데요, 양해해 주실 수 있는지 궁금합니다. 체크아웃 시간을 연장하고 오늘 늦게 계산하는 게 가능할까요? 사실, 제 비행편이 변경돼서 오늘밤에 떠나거든요.
접수원	얼마나 늦추실 건가요?
손님	아마 세 시간요. 그래서 체크아웃은 3시가 되겠네요.
접수원	괜찮을 것 같습니다.
손님	다행이네요. 감사합니다.

A
1 T
2 F
3 F
4 T

B
1 have a reservation
2 we have a table reserved
3 take your order
4 It comes with a salad
5 How would you like

C
1 to extend her check-out time
2 Her flight schedule has changed.
3 3 o'clock

SPECIAL PART — 비즈니스 이메일
Business E-mail

UNIT 01 비즈니스 이메일 보내기

Vocabulary Check-up p.125

1 Dear Mr.
2 My name is
3 in charge of
4 whom it may
5 look forward to

Writing Exercise p.128

A 1 My name is Jeongeun Kim, and I am in charge of the Marketing Department.
2 Our company specializes in household appliances.
3 I am e-mailing you regarding your complaint dated October 4.
4 If you have any further questions, please don't hesitate to contact the Personnel Department.
5 I'm looking forward to your prompt and positive response to our offer.
6 Should you wish to have further information regarding this matter
7 I am emailing you regarding some problems with my laptop computer.
8 We wish to provide you with some detailed information about our product.

B 1 regarding the matter you mentioned in your email from July 2.
2 I was given your name by
3 We wish to provide you with information on / do not hesitate to contact me

UNIT 02 첨부파일 보내기

Vocabulary Check-up p.131

1 acknowledgment email
2 am pleased to inform
3 for security purposes
4 after signing
5 experience any difficulties

Writing Exercise p.134

A 1 I am enclosing an attachment which contains all the information you requested.
2 I had to compress our new catalog as the size of the file is too big to send as is.
3 Please use an appropriate program to decompress it once you receive the file.
4 The contract that I sent you yesterday is in PDF format, so MS Word is not compatible with it.
5 Please accept my apologies for emailing you without the attachment I was supposed to enclose.
6 Please let me know if you have any problems opening the file that I sent you.
7 I am pleased to inform you that we have decided to accept your offer.
8 Please note that I will be out of the office for all of next week.

B 1 I am enclosing an attachment / compress our new catalog / use an appropriate program to decompress it
2 accept my apologies for / Please view it with / let me know if you have any problems
3 note that I will be out of the office from September 15, and I shall be back in the office by October 15

UNIT 03 미팅 약속 정하기

Vocabulary Check-up p.137

1 alternatively
2 set up an appointment
3 not be available
4 leave a message with
5 get back to

Writing Exercise p.140

A 1 I'd like to see you in person to discuss our next year's project if possible.
2 I will be free next Friday at 12 p.m.
3 3 o'clock on November 5 would be okay for me to meet you.
4 It would help me greatly if we met at the Grand Hotel on Wednesday the 13th.
5 I need to reschedule our meeting for another day.
6 I will be available on Wednesday from approximately 11 a.m. to 1 p.m.
7 I know I was supposed to meet you at 10 a.m., but something has come up.
8 Please let me know if you have a place in mind.

B 1 If it is possible / How about 3 o'clock on Tuesday / Let

me know

2 need to reschedule our meeting to another day / very sorry for any inconvenience

3 ask for additional information / get back to you by Tuesday

UNIT 04  동료 간의 인사 메일

Vocabulary Check-up p.143

1 was / impressed by

2 appreciate / how to

3 thoughtful of

4 Thank you again

5 could / have succeeded

6 took the position

Writing Exercise p.146

A 1 Thanks so much for being with us when you are busy.

2 I will be transferred to the Daejeon branch.

3 I heard you are having some problems.

4 I am sorry to say (that) I cannot come to the party.

5 I'd appreciate it if you could call me as soon as you get a chance.

6 I hear you've been promoted to section chief this time.

7 On behalf of our team, we wish you good luck in your retirement.

8 We would like to apologize for the delay in sending our engineers to your Incheon office.

B 1 Without your company, our company would have some big problems. / Thank you again for your help

2 I am going to be transferred to / My replacement will be / I will give you my new contact number later.

3 I apologize for the delay / We hope you'll enjoy it

English for Business Communication 시리즈

General Business   Practical Business   International Business

English for Business Communication 시리즈는 전 3권에 걸쳐 비즈니스 업무 진행에 필수적인 영어 표현들을 습득할 수 있도록 구성하였습니다.

General Business   비즈니스 일상 영어

출퇴근 인사를 비롯하여 동료 간의 커뮤니케이션을 위한 일상 표현들과, 비즈니스 업무의 기본인 전화 응대, 약속 잡기, 외국손님 맞이, 해외 출장 등에 관련한 영어 표현들을 익힙니다.

Practical Business   사내 실무 영어

좀 더 실질적인 업무 처리를 요하는 프레젠테이션 상황, 회의, 업무 지시 및 보고, 의견 제안 및 설득 등 효과적인 커뮤니케이션을 위한 핵심적인 영어 표현들을 다룹니다.

International Business   비즈니스 국제 영어

회사간 무역 거래, 계약 및 협상, 마케팅 협의, 재정 관리 등 대외적인 업무 처리에 필요한 영어 표현들을 익힙니다.

Overview

PART 1 비즈니스 회의 Business Meetings

Week	Title	Overview
WEEK 01	회의 소집 및 안건 소개 Calling a Meeting and Addressing the Agenda	회의 관련 기본 어휘 익히기 Learning basic vocabulary for meetings 회의 소집하기 Calling a meeting 안건 소개하기 Introducing agenda items
WEEK 02	안건 토의하기 Discussing the Agenda	효과적으로 회의 시작하기 Starting a meeting effectively 의견 말하기 Expressing opinions 안건에 대한 의견 묻기 Asking for opinions about the agenda
WEEK 03	회의 통제하기 및 끝맺기 Controlling and Wrapping up a Meeting	끼어드는 법 익히기 Learning how to interrupt 회의 통제하기 Controlling a meeting 요약하고 회의 끝맺기 Summarizing and wrapping up a meeting
PLUS WEEK	동의하기 및 반대하기 Agreeing and Disagreeing	동의 표시하기 Expressing agreement 반대 표시하기 Expressing disagreement 의견 강조하기 Emphasizing opinions

PART 2 비즈니스 프레젠테이션 Business Presentations

Week	Title	Overview
WEEK 04	발표 목적과 발표자 소개 Introducing the Goal of the Presentation and the Presenter	발표자 소개하기 Introducing a presenter 발표 목적 알리기 Informing about the purpose of the presentation 발표 절차 안내하기 Explaining the procedure of the presentation
WEEK 05	발표 시작과 전개 Starting and Developing a Presentation	효과적으로 발표 시작하기 Starting a presentation effectively 발표 전개하기 Developing a presentation 주제 전환하기 Switching topics
WEEK 06	발표 마무리하기 및 질문받기 Concluding a Presentation and Taking Questions	주요 사항 요약하기 Summarizing main points 발표 마무리하기 Concluding a presentation 질문에 답하기 Answering questions
PLUS WEEK	시각자료 사용 및 효과적인 분석 Visual Aids and Effective Analysis	시각자료 소개하기 Showing visual aids 효과적으로 자료 분석하기 Analyzing the visuals effectively 논리적으로 발표하기 Making logical presentations

SPECIAL PART 비즈니스 이메일 Business E-mail

Unit	Title	Overview
UNIT 01	의견 묻고 나누기 Asking and Sharing Opinions	의견 요청하기 Asking for opinions 의견 말하기 Giving opinions 의견 진술 회피하기 Avoiding giving opinions
UNIT 02	동의하기 또는 반대하기 Agreeing or Disagreeing	동의하기 Agreeing 반대하기 Disagreeing 대안 제시하기 Proposing alternatives

Overview

Part 1 국제 무역 International Trade

Week	Title	Overview
WEEK 01	제품 정보 얻기 Obtaining Information about Products	제품 사양에 대해 묻기 Asking about a product's specifications 제품 특징에 대해 말하기 Talking about a product's features 자료 요청하기 Requesting product information
WEEK 02	가격 인하 요청하기 Requesting a Price Reduction	가격에 대해 묻기 Asking about prices 가격 비교하기 Comparing prices 할인 요청하기 Asking for a discount
WEEK 03	주문과 배송 Order and Delivery	주문하기 Placing an order 제품 배송하기 Delivering products 품질보증에 대해 묻기 Asking about warranties
PLUS WEEK	클레임 처리하기 Dealing with Claims	불만 표시하기 Making complaints 고객 불만에 대처하기 Handling complaints 불만사항 해결하기 Solving complaints

Part 2 협상 Negotiation

Week	Title	Overview
WEEK 04	교섭자 맞이하기 Greeting Negotiators	소개하기 Making introductions 가벼운 이야기 나누기 Making small talk 협상 절차 설명하기 Explaining the negotiation procedure
WEEK 05	입장 밝히기 Establishing Positions	협상 안건 확인하기 Confirming the negotiation agenda 입장을 명확하게 취하기 Clarifying your position 입장 정리하기 Summarizing each position
WEEK 06	제안하기와 흥정하기 Making Proposals and Bargaining	제안하기 Making proposals 대안 제시하기 Making counterproposals 흥정하기 Bargaining
PLUS WEEK	갈등 대처하기와 협상 끝내기 Handling Conflicts and Closing a Negotiation	강력하게 주장하기 Insisting on your opinion 해결책 찾기 Creating solutions 계약 체결하기 Closing a contract

SPECIAL PART 비즈니스 이메일 Business E-mail

Unit	Title	Overview
UNIT 01	제품에 관한 문의 Questions about Products	제품 사양 설명하기 Explaining a product's specifications 카탈로그 및 견본 보내기 Sending catalogs and sample products
UNIT 02	주문하기 Placing an Order	주문하기 Placing an order 주문을 취소하거나 변경하기 Canceling or changing an order 선적 및 대금 정보 받기 Obtaining shipping/payment information

Part 3 마케팅 Marketing

Part 4 재정 및 금융 Money and Finance